Chapter 1: Introduction to Radio Frequency Technologies

Radio frequency (RF) technologies are an essential component of modern communication and technology. From the way we connect to the internet, to the GPS systems in our cars, and even the wireless devices that surround us, RF technologies form the backbone of a vast array of systems. RF encompasses a broad spectrum of electromagnetic waves, and understanding how these signals interact with the world around us is key to harnessing their full potential.

In this chapter, we'll explore the basics of RF technologies—what they are, how they work, and why controlling and manipulating RF signals is crucial for industries ranging from telecommunications to security and defense.

What are Radio Frequencies?

Radio frequency refers to the electromagnetic waves used for transmitting data and information over long distances. These waves, which have frequencies between 3 Hz and 300 GHz, are part of the broader electromagnetic spectrum, alongside visible light, infrared, X-rays, and other types of waves. RF waves are used in a variety of applications, including radio and television broadcasts, wireless communication, satellite links, and cellular networks.

The RF spectrum is divided into multiple bands, each of which serves a specific purpose. These bands are typically regulated by governmental organizations, such as the Federal Communications Commission (FCC) in the United States or the International Telecommunication Union (ITU) globally, to ensure that RF technologies do not interfere with each other.

The Importance of RF Technologies

RF technologies are at the core of virtually all wireless communication systems. In the modern world, RF signals enable seamless communication in everything from Wi-Fi networks and cellular phones to smart home devices and critical systems in the healthcare and transportation industries.

Wireless communication relies on the ability to transmit RF signals through the air. These signals are used to carry information, such as voice, data, and video, between devices. The efficiency, quality, and security of RF communication are highly dependent on controlling these signals and managing how they interact with the environment.

RF in Everyday Life

From the moment we wake up and check our phones to the time we fall asleep with a Wi-Fi-enabled device nearby, we are constantly surrounded by RF signals. The cell phone in your pocket, the Bluetooth speaker playing music, and even the radio stations broadcasting across the airwaves all use RF technology.

RF technology is also used in more critical applications, such as medical devices that monitor vital signs, GPS systems that navigate our vehicles, and emergency response systems that help coordinate rescue efforts in times of crisis.

The pervasive presence of RF signals in modern life means that managing and understanding these frequencies is not only important for technological innovation but also for safeguarding against interference, security risks, and health concerns.

Challenges of RF Signals

Despite the many benefits of RF technology, there are several challenges associated with its use. As more devices rely on RF signals for communication, the RF spectrum has become increasingly congested. This results in potential interference, where signals from different sources overlap or interfere with one another, reducing the quality and reliability of communication systems.

In addition to interference, RF signals can also have unintended effects on devices, individuals, and environments. For example, excessive exposure to RF radiation can cause heating effects in biological tissues, leading to health concerns. To mitigate these risks, proper shielding and filtering of RF signals are necessary.

Furthermore, in sensitive environments—such as military, government, or industrial settings—unauthorized access to RF signals can pose serious security threats. Signals can be intercepted, jammed, or manipulated to gain access to sensitive data or disrupt critical systems. In these contexts, controlling RF signals is a matter of national security, operational efficiency, and safety.

The Need for RF Shielding and Control

Given the potential for interference, security threats, and health concerns, there is a growing need for effective RF shielding and control. Shielding and absorption technologies are essential for isolating sensitive systems from unwanted RF signals. Techniques such as anti-RF technology, RF filtering, and the use of white noise can help control RF signals to ensure their proper functioning and mitigate potential risks.

RF shielding, which prevents or reduces the amount of RF energy that enters or leaves a space, is essential for protecting sensitive electronic equipment from external interference. Anti-RF technology aims to block or disrupt unwanted RF signals, while RF filters help eliminate specific frequencies to allow only the desired signals to pass through. White noise, on the other hand, is used to mask or obscure RF signals, providing an additional layer of security or interference prevention.

This book will explore these techniques in detail, offering insights into how they work, when to use them, and how to integrate them into various systems. Whether you're working with consumer electronics, military applications, or telecommunications, understanding RF shielding is critical for ensuring the reliability, security, and safety of RF-dependent technologies.

A Snapshot of RF Shielding Technologies

As we delve deeper into the subject of RF shielding, we'll explore the key methods and materials used to control RF signals:

- **RF Absorption**: The process of capturing and converting RF energy into heat using materials that absorb electromagnetic waves. This is a critical component in reducing interference and ensuring device performance.
- **Anti-RF Technology**: A set of techniques designed to block or neutralize unwanted RF signals, such as jamming and countermeasures against signal interception.
- **RF Filtering**: The use of filters to allow only specific RF frequencies to pass through, ensuring that unwanted signals are blocked, and the intended signals remain intact.
- **White Noise**: A random signal that can mask or disrupt RF signals, often used to secure communication channels or protect sensitive systems from interception.

These techniques form the core of modern RF shielding strategies, and mastering them is essential for anyone working in environments that rely on RF technologies.

Conclusion

RF technology plays an increasingly vital role in modern life, from everyday consumer devices to critical communication systems in business, healthcare, and defense. As the use of wireless technology expands, understanding how to manage RF signals—through absorption, filtering, and shielding techniques—becomes essential for maintaining signal integrity, preventing interference, and ensuring the security of sensitive information.

This chapter has introduced the fundamental concepts of RF technology and set the stage for a deeper exploration of the tools and techniques used to master RF shielding. In the chapters that follow, we will delve into the science of RF absorption, the principles behind anti-RF technology, the different types of RF filters, and the strategic use of white noise to protect and control RF signals.

This first chapter sets the stage for a comprehensive journey into mastering RF shielding and the technologies that empower it. Through understanding the foundational principles of RF signals and their challenges, readers can begin to grasp the importance of controlling these frequencies in various applications.

Chapter 2: Understanding Radio Frequencies and Their Impact

Radio frequencies (RF) are electromagnetic waves that span a broad range of the electromagnetic spectrum, and they are integral to numerous technologies that drive modern communication systems. Understanding how RF signals behave and interact with the world around us is essential for effectively controlling them in various applications, from consumer electronics to military and security systems.

In this chapter, we will explore the fundamentals of RF, how RF signals are generated and transmitted, their interactions with different materials, and the impact these signals can have on both technology and health. By the end of this chapter, readers will have a deeper understanding of the RF spectrum, the factors that influence RF propagation, and the consequences of poor RF management.

What is Radio Frequency?

Radio frequency refers to the range of electromagnetic waves that fall between 3 Hz and 300 GHz, and these frequencies are primarily used for wireless communication. RF signals are created by oscillating electric and magnetic fields that propagate through space as electromagnetic waves. These waves can carry information such as voice, data, and video, and are the backbone of technologies such as radio, television, satellite communications, Wi-Fi, and cellular networks.

RF signals are characterized by their frequency, which is the number of cycles the wave completes in one second, measured in Hertz (Hz). The higher the frequency, the shorter the wavelength. The RF spectrum is divided into several frequency bands, each with distinct characteristics and uses. Some of the most common RF bands include:

- **Low Frequency (LF)**: 30-300 kHz
- **Medium Frequency (MF)**: 300 kHz to 3 MHz
- **High Frequency (HF)**: 3 MHz to 30 MHz
- **Very High Frequency (VHF)**: 30 MHz to 300 MHz
- **Ultra High Frequency (UHF)**: 300 MHz to 3 GHz
- **Super High Frequency (SHF)**: 3 GHz to 30 GHz
- **Extremely High Frequency (EHF)**: 30 GHz to 300 GHz

Each of these frequency ranges serves different purposes, from AM radio broadcasts (typically in the MF range) to microwave transmissions (in the SHF and EHF ranges) that are used for radar, satellite communication, and 5G technology.

How RF Signals are Generated and Transmitted

RF signals are generated by oscillators or transmitters, which produce alternating currents at specific frequencies. These signals are then transmitted through antennas, which radiate the RF energy into the air. The transmission of RF signals follows the principles of electromagnetic wave propagation, which are influenced by factors such as the frequency of the wave, the environment through which it travels, and the design of the antenna.

Once an RF signal leaves the transmitter, it can travel in several different ways, depending on the frequency and surrounding conditions. The signal may propagate through free space, reflect off surfaces, refract through different media, or be absorbed by obstacles in its path. These propagation effects are important to consider when designing communication systems, as they influence the quality and range of the transmitted signal.

Factors Affecting RF Signal Propagation

RF signal propagation is influenced by several key factors, including:

- **Frequency**: Higher frequencies generally have shorter wavelengths, which means they tend to travel shorter distances and are more likely to be blocked or absorbed by obstacles. Lower frequencies, on the other hand, tend to travel further and can penetrate solid objects more effectively.

- **Obstacles and Environment**: Physical objects, such as buildings, trees, and mountains, can cause RF signals to reflect, diffract, or scatter. This can lead to signal degradation and interference. In urban environments, signals may face higher levels of obstruction due to tall buildings, which can create "shadow zones" where RF signals are weakened or blocked entirely.

- **Atmospheric Conditions**: The Earth's atmosphere can have varying effects on RF signals, especially at higher frequencies. For example, moisture, rain, and snow can cause attenuation (signal weakening) of signals, particularly in the microwave and millimeter-wave ranges.

- **Antenna Design and Placement**: The performance of an RF system is significantly influenced by the design of the antenna and its placement. Antennas are engineered to emit or receive signals at specific frequencies, and their orientation and height can impact the range and quality of the signal.

Impact of RF Signals on Technology

The ability to control and manipulate RF signals is central to the operation of modern communication systems. For example, in wireless communication, such as Wi-Fi or cellular networks, RF signals are used to transmit data between devices, allowing for efficient, high-speed information transfer. When RF signals are properly managed, communication systems can operate with minimal interference and maximum efficiency.

However, the behavior of RF signals can also present challenges. In dense environments with a high concentration of RF devices—such as cities, office buildings, or even large factory floors—RF interference can occur when signals from different devices overlap. This interference can cause degradation in the performance of communication systems, resulting in slower data rates, dropped connections, or complete system failures.

Additionally, RF signals can impact the functionality of sensitive electronic equipment. For example, unintended RF interference can disrupt the operation of medical devices, such as pacemakers or MRI machines, or industrial equipment used in critical systems like manufacturing or transportation. This has led to the development of stringent regulations around the use of RF devices and the design of RF-sensitive environments.

Health Impacts of RF Exposure

There has been ongoing research into the potential health effects of exposure to RF radiation. While RF signals are non-ionizing (meaning they do not have enough energy to remove electrons from atoms or molecules), prolonged or intense exposure can still cause thermal effects. These effects occur when the energy from RF waves is absorbed by the body and converted into heat, potentially leading to tissue damage.

Common concerns about RF exposure have been raised regarding devices such as mobile phones, which emit RF energy when transmitting and receiving signals. The potential for long-term health effects, including cancer, has been a subject of debate, though the scientific consensus remains that there is no conclusive evidence linking low-level RF exposure to adverse health outcomes. Regulatory bodies such as the World Health Organization (WHO) and the Federal Communications Commission (FCC) set safety standards to limit RF exposure and protect public health.

Despite these concerns, the general consensus is that properly shielded and regulated RF devices do not pose significant health risks. Nonetheless, it remains essential to monitor RF exposure and minimize excessive exposure in environments where people are frequently exposed to RF signals.

The Need for RF Management

Given the pervasive nature of RF signals and their impact on both technology and health, managing RF signals effectively is critical for the smooth operation of communication systems and for minimizing interference. As RF technology continues to evolve, particularly with the advent of 5G and the expansion of IoT (Internet of Things) networks, the demand for robust RF management will only increase.

Proper RF management involves a variety of strategies, including:

- **Shielding and Absorption**: Techniques to protect sensitive equipment and individuals from unwanted RF signals.
- **Filtering**: Implementing filters to isolate or block unwanted frequencies.
- **Interference Mitigation**: Identifying sources of interference and employing solutions such as jamming, frequency hopping, and the use of white noise.

In the chapters that follow, we will delve deeper into these techniques, exploring how to design and implement effective RF shielding and filtering systems, as well as how to use advanced technologies such as white noise to manage RF interference.

Conclusion

Understanding the nature of RF signals, their behavior, and the factors that influence their propagation is the first step toward mastering RF shielding technologies. The complexities of the RF spectrum, combined with the challenges of interference, signal degradation, and health concerns, make it essential for engineers, designers, and operators to have a deep understanding of RF management.

In the next chapter, we will dive into the science behind RF absorption and explore how different materials and techniques can be used to control RF signals, ensuring optimal performance and safety in a wide range of applications.

Chapter 4: Types of RF Absorption Materials

RF absorption is a critical component in the control and mitigation of unwanted electromagnetic interference (EMI). As discussed in the previous chapter, RF signals can interfere with sensitive equipment, degrade performance, and cause security risks. To manage these signals, RF absorption materials play an important role by capturing and dissipating the energy of RF waves, reducing the unwanted effects on surrounding environments and systems.

In this chapter, we will explore the different types of RF absorption materials, how they work, and the applications in which they are most effective. By understanding the properties and characteristics of these materials, we can make informed decisions on their use in various shielding and absorption systems.

What Makes a Material an Effective RF Absorber?

The effectiveness of an RF absorption material is determined by its ability to absorb electromagnetic energy at specific frequencies. This is achieved through the material's electrical and magnetic properties, which allow it to interact with the RF waves and convert the energy into heat, thereby dissipating the wave's energy and reducing its impact.

The key factors that influence a material's effectiveness as an RF absorber include:

- **Dielectric Constant**: A material's ability to store electrical energy in an electric field, which affects how it interacts with electromagnetic waves.
- **Magnetic Permeability**: A measure of a material's ability to conduct magnetic fields, influencing the absorption of magnetic components of RF signals.
- **Conductivity**: The ability of a material to conduct electricity, which affects its ability to dissipate the absorbed RF energy as heat.
- **Thickness and Frequency Range**: The thickness of the material and the specific frequencies it is designed to absorb determine its performance across the RF spectrum. For maximum effectiveness, the material must be designed to absorb the target frequency range.

Common Types of RF Absorption Materials

Carbon-Based Materials

Applications

Ferrites

Applications

Magnetic Materials (Metals)

Applications

Conductive Polymers

Applications

Metallo-Dielectric Materials

Applications

Foams and Fibrous Materials

Applications

Performance Criteria for RF Absorption Materials

When selecting materials for RF absorption, several performance criteria must be considered:

- **Absorption Efficiency**: The efficiency with which the material absorbs RF energy. This is typically measured as the material's reflection loss, which is the amount of energy reflected back from the material, and absorption loss, which is the energy converted into heat.
- **Frequency Range**: Different materials are effective over different frequency ranges. Some materials are better suited for high-frequency applications, while others excel at lower frequencies. Ensuring that the material is effective for the intended frequency range is crucial.
- **Thickness**: The thickness of the material is a critical factor in its ability to absorb RF energy. Generally, thicker materials can absorb more energy, but they may also be heavier and more difficult to implement in certain designs.
- **Durability**: The long-term stability and durability of RF absorption materials are essential, especially in harsh environments. Materials must be resistant to environmental factors such as temperature fluctuations, humidity, and mechanical wear.
- **Cost and Availability**: The cost-effectiveness and availability of materials are important considerations. While high-performance materials like ferrites and carbon composites may provide excellent absorption, they can be costly and may not be necessary for all applications.

Applications of RF Absorption Materials

The use of RF absorption materials spans a wide range of industries and applications. Here are some of the key areas where RF absorbers are utilized:

- **Electromagnetic Compatibility (EMC) and EMI Shielding**: RF absorption materials are frequently used in electronics to prevent electromagnetic interference. By absorbing unwanted signals, these materials help ensure that devices operate without disrupting other nearby electronics.
- **Military and Defense**: In military applications, RF absorption materials are used in radar-absorbing materials (RAM) to reduce the visibility of military vehicles, aircraft, and ships to radar systems. The goal is to create stealth technologies that absorb radar signals, making the target less detectable.
- **Consumer Electronics**: In everyday devices such as smartphones, laptops, and televisions, RF absorption materials help reduce interference from external signals and prevent RF leakage, improving the performance and longevity of these devices.
- **Automotive Industry**: With the rise of wireless connectivity in vehicles, RF absorption materials are used to reduce the effects of RF interference between the vehicle's internal systems, such as GPS, Bluetooth, and infotainment systems.
- **Aerospace and Space Applications**: In aerospace, RF absorbers are used to protect sensitive equipment from external RF signals, such as cosmic radiation or signals from other spacecraft, which can interfere with navigation, communication, and instrumentation systems.

Conclusion

RF absorption materials play a vital role in controlling electromagnetic interference and ensuring the reliability and functionality of a wide range of electronic systems. Whether in military applications, consumer electronics, or communication systems, the ability to absorb and dissipate unwanted RF energy is crucial for optimizing performance, protecting sensitive equipment, and improving system security.

In the next chapter, we will explore how to design and implement effective RF absorption systems, combining different materials and techniques to create solutions tailored to specific applications and environments.

Chapter 5: Designing Effective RF Absorption Systems

In the previous chapters, we discussed the science behind RF absorption and explored various materials used for absorbing RF signals. The next logical step is understanding how to design effective RF absorption systems that can be applied in real-world scenarios. The design of these systems is critical for mitigating electromagnetic interference (EMI) and ensuring the smooth operation of electronic systems, particularly in environments with high RF activity.

In this chapter, we will explore the key principles and considerations involved in designing effective RF absorption systems. This includes selecting the right materials, optimizing their placement, and ensuring that the system provides maximum attenuation for specific frequencies. By the end of this chapter, readers will have a clear understanding of how to design and implement RF absorption solutions that are both efficient and practical for a variety of applications.

Key Design Principles for RF Absorption Systems

Designing an RF absorption system requires a deep understanding of both the RF environment and the specific requirements of the equipment being protected or shielded. The following are the key principles that guide the design of effective RF absorption systems:

1. **Frequency Range**: The first step in designing an RF absorption system is understanding the frequency range of the signals that need to be absorbed. RF signals vary widely in frequency, and the effectiveness of a material depends on how well it can absorb energy at the specific frequencies of concern. For example, materials that absorb low-frequency signals may not be effective at high frequencies, and vice versa. Designers need to ensure that the absorption materials chosen are suited to the target frequency range.

2. **Material Selection**: As covered in Chapter 4, there are a variety of materials that can be used to absorb RF energy. Each material has its strengths and weaknesses, so selecting the right material depends on the specific application, the frequency of the signals, the required absorption level, and other factors such as cost and availability. Combining different materials in a multi-layer design can often improve performance by taking advantage of the unique properties of each material.

3. **Thickness and Layering**: The thickness of the absorbing material plays a crucial role in the system's overall performance. Thicker materials generally provide better absorption, but they can also increase the weight and bulk of the system. Multi-layer designs, where different materials are stacked to provide enhanced absorption across a broader frequency spectrum, can be more effective in many situations. Each layer should be optimized to absorb a specific frequency range, creating a system that is efficient at attenuating a wide range of RF signals.

4. **Design Geometry and Placement**: The placement and geometry of the absorption materials are just as important as the material itself. The layout of the shielding system should be carefully designed to ensure that RF signals are directed toward the absorption materials and that these materials cover the areas most at risk for interference. In many cases, the absorption materials must be placed around sensitive equipment or inside enclosures to protect against external RF signals.

5. **Environmental Considerations**: RF absorption systems must be designed with the operating environment in mind. Factors such as temperature, humidity, mechanical stress, and exposure to chemicals or other harsh conditions can impact the performance of the absorption materials. For example, materials that work well in a dry indoor environment may not perform effectively in a high-humidity environment or at extreme temperatures. It is essential to select materials that will perform consistently in the expected conditions.

Designing RF Absorption Systems for Specific Applications

Different applications require tailored approaches to RF absorption system design. Here, we will explore how RF absorption systems are designed for several key industries:

1. **Consumer Electronics**: In consumer electronics such as smartphones, tablets, and laptops, RF absorption is crucial for ensuring that RF signals do not interfere with the operation of the device or with other nearby devices. Absorption systems in these applications must be lightweight, compact, and effective at higher frequencies, such as those used for Wi-Fi, Bluetooth, and cellular communication. A common approach in these devices is using thin layers of conductive materials like graphene or carbon nanotubes that absorb RF energy while adding minimal bulk.

2. **Automotive Industry**: With the proliferation of connected vehicles and the increasing number of wireless systems in cars (including GPS, wireless charging, and communication networks), RF absorption is necessary to prevent interference between these systems. RF absorption systems in automotive applications need to be robust, lightweight, and resistant to environmental factors like temperature changes, moisture, and vibration. Automotive RF absorption solutions often use composite materials that combine carbon-based polymers with metal particles, providing effective RF absorption while maintaining the integrity of the vehicle's structure.

3. **Aerospace and Defense**: The aerospace and defense industries require highly effective RF absorption systems to shield sensitive equipment from RF interference, particularly in high-frequency bands used by radar, communication systems, and other critical electronics. RF absorption materials in these applications must be able to handle extreme environmental conditions, including high-altitude pressure, extreme temperatures, and exposure to radiation. Materials such as ferrites and magnetic metals are often used in aerospace applications, along with specialized RAM (radar-absorbing materials) designed to minimize the radar signature of military vehicles and aircraft.

4. **Healthcare**: In medical environments, RF interference can disrupt the operation of critical medical devices such as pacemakers, MRI machines, and other life-saving technologies. RF absorption systems are designed to protect these devices from external interference and ensure that the devices themselves do not emit harmful RF signals that could affect nearby equipment. Materials that provide high attenuation of RF energy, such as specialized conductive polymers and metallic foams, are commonly used in these applications.

5. **Industrial and Commercial Systems**: In industrial environments where machinery and sensitive electronics coexist, RF interference can be a significant issue. RF absorption systems must be designed to protect industrial equipment from external RF signals, while also minimizing interference from the machinery itself. Large-scale industrial systems often use layered absorption systems made from materials such as ferrite tiles, carbon-loaded foams, and conductive paints to absorb RF energy efficiently and cost-effectively.

Advanced Techniques for Enhancing RF Absorption Performance

In addition to the basic design principles, there are several advanced techniques that can be employed to enhance the performance of RF absorption systems:

1. **Metamaterials**: Metamaterials are engineered materials that possess properties not found in naturally occurring materials. These materials can be designed to exhibit unique electromagnetic characteristics, such as negative refraction, which can enhance RF absorption and provide more targeted attenuation across specific frequencies. Metamaterials are being increasingly researched for their potential to improve RF shielding and absorption performance, especially in applications that require highly selective absorption at particular frequencies.
2. **Frequency Selective Surfaces (FSS)**: Frequency selective surfaces are periodic structures that allow certain frequencies to pass through while absorbing or reflecting others. These surfaces are used in advanced RF absorption systems to selectively absorb energy at specific frequencies while allowing other frequencies to propagate through. FSS can be applied in antenna design, radar systems, and other applications where precise control of RF energy is needed.
3. **Active Absorption Systems**: While most RF absorption systems rely on passive materials to absorb RF energy, active absorption systems use electronically controlled elements such as diodes, transistors, or tunable capacitors to dynamically adjust the absorption properties of the system. Active systems can adapt to changing RF environments, making them highly effective in environments where the frequency and intensity of RF signals fluctuate.

4. **Hybrid Absorption Systems**: Hybrid systems combine multiple absorption techniques and materials to create a more efficient and versatile solution. For example, a hybrid absorption system might use ferrites for low-frequency absorption, carbon-based materials for higher frequencies, and active elements to provide dynamic adjustment. These systems are particularly useful in complex environments where RF signals vary widely in frequency and intensity.

Conclusion

Designing effective RF absorption systems requires a comprehensive understanding of the materials, frequency ranges, and environmental factors that influence RF signals. Whether for consumer electronics, military applications, or industrial environments, the right RF absorption solution can prevent interference, protect sensitive equipment, and ensure that systems operate optimally.

In the next chapter, we will explore the principles of anti-RF technology and how it is used to actively block or disrupt unwanted RF signals. Understanding both passive absorption and active RF blocking technologies provides a complete toolkit for mastering RF shielding and managing RF interference.

Chapter 6: Principles of Anti-RF Technology

Anti-RF technology is a powerful tool used to block or neutralize unwanted radio frequency (RF) signals. Unlike passive RF absorption, which absorbs and dissipates RF energy, anti-RF technology actively interferes with or obstructs RF signals to prevent their transmission or reception. This can be crucial in environments where unwanted RF interference could cause disruption, security breaches, or signal degradation.

In this chapter, we will explore the fundamental principles of anti-RF technology, the methods used to block or disrupt RF signals, and how these technologies are applied in real-world scenarios. By understanding the mechanics of anti-RF systems, you will be better equipped to design solutions that safeguard systems from unwanted RF signals and enhance overall security.

What is Anti-RF Technology?

Anti-RF technology refers to systems or techniques specifically designed to block, jam, or otherwise prevent the transmission of RF signals. This can be achieved through various methods, including the use of jammers, frequency-hopping technologies, or deliberate interference. Anti-RF technologies are often used in military, law enforcement, and high-security environments where preventing unauthorized communication or protecting sensitive information is paramount.

The primary goal of anti-RF technology is to disrupt or block unwanted RF signals without causing harm to the surrounding environment or legitimate communication systems. This requires precise control over which signals are targeted and how interference is applied.

Principles of Anti-RF Technology

The effectiveness of anti-RF technology is based on several key principles that govern how RF signals propagate, interact with materials, and can be disrupted:

Signal Jamming

Types of Jamming

- **Continuous Wave (CW) Jamming**: The jammer continuously emits a signal on the target frequency.
- **Burst Jamming**: The jammer emits a burst of interference at random intervals, making it more difficult for the target signal to regain clarity.
- **Frequency Jamming**: The jammer targets a specific frequency band, preventing communication on that band while allowing other frequencies to operate.
- **Spot Jamming**: A highly focused and powerful jamming technique that targets a specific signal of interest.

Signal Spoofing

GPS Spoofing

Frequency Hopping

Applications

Directional Antennas

Applications

Shielding and Faraday Cages

Applications

Rejection of Harmonics and Spurious Emissions

Applications

Applications of Anti-RF Devices

The application of anti-RF technology is vast and varied, with the most common uses being in military, security, and communication sectors. Some of the most notable applications include:

1. **Military and Defense**:

   Anti-RF technology is essential in military operations where secure communication and protection against enemy electronic warfare are critical. Jamming is frequently used to block enemy communications or disrupt radar systems. Spoofing is also employed to mislead adversary navigation systems. In addition, anti-RF devices are used to shield military vehicles, drones, and other equipment from detection by enemy radar.

2. **Security and Law Enforcement**:

   Anti-RF technology is used to safeguard sensitive areas, such as government buildings, data centers, and financial institutions. Signal jamming can prevent unauthorized access to wireless communication systems, while shielding techniques protect against eavesdropping. In law enforcement, anti-RF technology is used to counteract threats posed by remote detonation devices or unauthorized surveillance systems.

3. **Industrial Applications**:

   In industrial settings, RF interference can cause malfunctions in machinery or disrupt critical processes. Anti-RF devices help protect sensitive equipment from unintended electromagnetic interference. For example, in factories where precision machinery and robotics are used, jamming and shielding are employed to prevent RF signals from disrupting the operation.

4. **Telecommunications**:

    Anti-RF technologies are used by telecom companies to ensure that communication networks remain secure and operational. Frequency hopping and other methods are applied to prevent eavesdropping and to improve the resilience of the network against signal interference.

5. **Consumer Electronics**:

    In consumer electronics, anti-RF technology is used to prevent interference between devices, ensuring that they operate smoothly in a crowded RF environment. For instance, RF interference between devices in a smart home can be mitigated using anti-RF technology to maintain clear communication channels.

Challenges in Implementing Anti-RF Technology

While anti-RF technology offers powerful solutions for protecting against RF interference and enhancing security, there are several challenges in its implementation:

- **Regulatory Constraints**: In many countries, the use of jamming technology is heavily regulated or even illegal, as it can interfere with civilian communication systems, such as emergency services and aviation. Operators must ensure that anti-RF systems comply with local regulations to avoid legal consequences.
- **Unintended Consequences**: Overuse or improper application of anti-RF technology can have unintended side effects, such as disrupting legitimate communication networks or interfering with public safety systems. This requires careful planning and coordination to ensure that only the intended targets are affected.
- **Cost and Complexity**: Developing and deploying effective anti-RF systems can be costly and technically complex. Factors such as signal range, power requirements, and adaptability to changing environments must be carefully considered when designing these systems.

Conclusion

Anti-RF technology is an essential tool in modern RF shielding strategies, particularly for environments where protecting sensitive systems and preventing unauthorized communication are paramount. By understanding the principles behind anti-RF technologies and their applications, you can better design systems that safeguard against RF interference and enhance security.

In the next chapter, we will explore the various applications of anti-RF devices in real-world settings, including military, security, and telecommunications, to understand how these technologies are deployed and the challenges they address.

Chapter 7: Applications of Anti-RF Devices

Anti-RF devices play a crucial role in a wide range of industries and sectors, from national security to commercial communication systems. The ability to block, disrupt, or neutralize unwanted RF signals is indispensable in environments where signal integrity, privacy, and protection from external threats are critical. This chapter explores the various applications of anti-RF technology, highlighting how these devices are deployed in military, security, telecommunications, industrial settings, and consumer electronics.

1. Military and Defense Applications

Anti-RF technology has its roots in military and defense applications, where the need for secure communications, protection against electronic warfare, and defense against surveillance is paramount. The primary focus of anti-RF devices in the military is to ensure that friendly forces maintain operational security while denying adversaries access to crucial communication channels or radar systems.

- **Signal Jamming and Interception**: Anti-RF technology is heavily used in military operations to prevent enemy communication and disrupt adversarial radar systems. Signal jammers are deployed to block or disrupt the enemy's ability to communicate, making it difficult for them to coordinate attacks or relay intelligence. In addition to tactical field operations, anti-RF systems are used in naval and air defense applications to neutralize hostile radar and missile targeting systems.
- **GPS Spoofing and Navigation Protection**: GPS systems are essential for modern military navigation, but they are also vulnerable to spoofing (i.e., providing false signals to mislead navigation systems). Anti-RF technology is employed to protect friendly GPS systems from such spoofing attempts, ensuring that navigation remains accurate during critical operations.
- **Radar Absorption and Stealth Technology**: Anti-RF devices in the form of radar-absorbing materials (RAM) are employed to reduce the visibility of military vehicles, aircraft, and ships to enemy radar. These materials absorb or scatter radar waves, minimizing the reflection of signals and making it harder for the enemy to detect or track military assets. RAM is crucial in stealth technology, which seeks to make military equipment undetectable by radar.

- **Electronic Countermeasures (ECM)**: Anti-RF technology is used in electronic warfare to neutralize the effectiveness of enemy weapons. ECM systems target enemy radar, communications, and guidance systems by emitting disruptive signals or jamming them. These systems are vital for ensuring the safety of military forces and preventing the enemy from gaining an upper hand through advanced technologies.

2. Security and Law Enforcement

Anti-RF technology is also indispensable in protecting sensitive locations and maintaining national security. Security agencies, including law enforcement and intelligence organizations, use anti-RF systems to prevent unauthorized communication, protect confidential information, and disrupt criminal activities.

- **Jamming Unauthorized Communication**: Anti-RF devices are used by security forces to block the communications of unauthorized individuals, including terrorists, criminals, or unauthorized drones. For instance, in prisons, anti-RF devices are deployed to prevent inmates from using contraband cell phones or other communication devices to plan escapes or coordinate criminal activities.
- **Protecting Critical Infrastructure**: Anti-RF technology helps protect vital infrastructure, such as government buildings, data centers, and military installations. These devices are used to prevent unauthorized surveillance, interference, or hacking attempts that might exploit wireless communication systems. For instance, RF jamming can protect high-security locations from espionage or unauthorized RF signal detection.
- **Drone Disruption**: Drones equipped with RF transmitters can pose significant security risks, especially when used to smuggle contraband, carry out surveillance, or deliver payloads to restricted areas. Anti-RF technology can be deployed to jam or spoof drone communications, rendering them incapable of carrying out their missions.

3. Telecommunications and Broadcasting

In telecommunications and broadcasting, anti-RF devices are used to maintain signal integrity, ensure compliance with regulatory requirements, and protect communication networks from interference or eavesdropping.

- **Signal Protection and Interference Prevention**: Telecommunication networks rely on RF signals for communication. Anti-RF devices are used to prevent interference from unauthorized sources or competing signal transmissions. These technologies help protect data integrity and prevent signal degradation, which can impact the reliability and security of communication services.
- **Preventing Eavesdropping**: Anti-RF devices are used to protect sensitive conversations from unauthorized interception. In industries like finance, healthcare, and government, the need to safeguard confidential information is paramount. Anti-RF systems can be used in secure meeting rooms or offices to block RF signals and prevent eavesdropping on private communications.
- **RF Filtering in Broadcasting**: In broadcasting, anti-RF technology ensures that signals are transmitted without interference. It can also be used to isolate specific frequencies for broadcasting purposes while preventing unwanted RF signals from interfering with broadcast quality.

4. Industrial Applications

In industrial settings, anti-RF technology is deployed to prevent RF interference that could disrupt manufacturing processes, sensitive measurements, or equipment performance. These systems are particularly important in environments where precise operation and minimal disruption are critical.

- **Manufacturing and Automation**: Many industrial processes, including automated manufacturing lines and robotic systems, rely on wireless communication for remote control and monitoring. Anti-RF systems are used to protect these processes from unintended interference, ensuring that machines operate without disruption. Additionally, RF shielding and filtering prevent equipment malfunction caused by external RF signals.
- **Protecting Industrial Equipment**: In sectors such as oil and gas, power generation, and chemical plants, industrial equipment can be sensitive to RF interference. Anti-RF technology helps shield sensitive machinery from RF signals that could impact their performance. This includes protecting equipment such as control systems, sensors, and instrumentation from disturbances caused by external wireless communications.
- **Industrial IoT Devices**: The industrial Internet of Things (IoT) relies heavily on wireless communication between devices. Anti-RF devices are used to maintain the integrity of communication between IoT sensors and controllers, especially in environments with high RF activity.

5. Consumer Electronics

In the consumer electronics sector, anti-RF technology is used to mitigate interference between devices, ensure signal integrity, and prevent potential health concerns from prolonged RF exposure. Many consumer devices, including smartphones, laptops, and wearables, are designed with anti-RF features to enhance performance and protect users.

- **Smartphone and Device Shielding**: Smartphones, laptops, and other portable electronic devices generate and receive RF signals. Anti-RF technology is incorporated into these devices to prevent RF interference with other equipment and to ensure compliance with regulatory standards regarding RF emissions. Shielding materials are often integrated into device enclosures to prevent external interference.

- **Health and Safety**: While the general scientific consensus maintains that RF exposure from consumer devices is safe at typical exposure levels, some users remain concerned about potential long-term effects. Manufacturers may incorporate anti-RF shielding in consumer devices to reduce RF emissions and address health concerns. This is especially true for products used close to the body, such as wearable devices.

- **Interference Prevention in Home Networks**: With the proliferation of smart homes and IoT devices, anti-RF technology is used to minimize interference between connected devices in the home. Smart home systems rely on wireless communication protocols such as Wi-Fi, Zigbee, and Bluetooth. Anti-RF devices help ensure that these devices communicate effectively without experiencing interference from other household electronics or external RF sources.

Challenges in Deploying Anti-RF Technology

While anti-RF technology has proven to be essential in various sectors, its implementation comes with challenges. These include:

- **Legal and Regulatory Considerations**: The use of signal jammers and RF interference devices is heavily regulated in many countries due to the potential for disrupting legitimate communication systems. In most regions, jamming technologies are only allowed for specific purposes, such as in military and law enforcement contexts. Organizations deploying anti-RF systems must ensure they comply with all applicable laws and regulations.
- **Unintended Consequences**: The use of anti-RF technology must be carefully controlled, as jamming or spoofing signals can interfere with critical services, including emergency communications, aviation systems, and other public safety networks. It is important to ensure that anti-RF systems do not inadvertently disrupt vital communication channels.
- **Cost and Complexity**: Developing and implementing anti-RF systems can be costly and technically complex. The equipment, materials, and expertise required to design and deploy effective anti-RF solutions can be significant, especially for large-scale applications or highly secure environments.

Conclusion

Anti-RF devices are an indispensable part of modern security, defense, telecommunications, and industrial systems. Their ability to block, disrupt, or neutralize unwanted RF signals ensures the integrity of communications, protects sensitive information, and mitigates the risks posed by RF interference. By understanding the diverse applications of anti-RF technology and the challenges associated with its deployment, organizations can better protect their operations from RF-related threats and ensure the safe and secure use of wireless technologies.

In the next chapter, we will explore how anti-RF technology can be integrated into building and installing comprehensive shielding solutions, creating systems that safeguard against RF interference while optimizing performance.

Chapter 8: Building and Installing Anti-RF Shielding

The effectiveness of anti-RF technology hinges on its ability to block, neutralize, or disrupt unwanted RF signals. One of the most fundamental approaches to ensuring that RF interference is minimized or completely eliminated is through the installation of anti-RF shielding. This shielding serves as a barrier that prevents the transmission or reception of RF energy, offering protection to sensitive electronic systems and securing environments where RF signals could compromise performance or security.

In this chapter, we will dive deep into the process of building and installing anti-RF shielding. We will explore the key principles behind its design, the materials used, and the installation methods that ensure maximum effectiveness. By understanding these processes, you will be able to design and implement anti-RF shielding systems that meet the needs of both critical infrastructure and everyday consumer electronics.

What is Anti-RF Shielding?

Anti-RF shielding involves the use of materials and techniques designed to block or reduce the penetration of electromagnetic waves (RF signals) into or out of a designated area. This type of shielding can protect sensitive equipment from external RF interference or prevent signals emitted from devices within an area from radiating outward and being intercepted. The goal is to create an environment where RF signals are contained or disrupted as needed to ensure the secure operation of electronic systems.

Anti-RF shielding is vital in environments where RF signals could compromise security, functionality, or the safety of users. This includes applications in military and defense, secure communications, medical devices, industrial automation, and consumer electronics.

Principles of Anti-RF Shielding Design

When designing anti-RF shielding systems, there are several principles that must be taken into account to ensure that the system performs as intended:

1. **Material Selection**:

   The choice of shielding material is critical to the success of the design. Different materials have different properties that affect their ability to block or absorb RF signals. Conductive metals like copper, aluminum, and steel are commonly used for their excellent electrical conductivity and ability to form effective barriers against RF waves. Additionally, ferrites, carbon-based materials, and specialized polymers can be used in combination with metals to enhance shielding performance, particularly for higher-frequency signals.

2. **Shielding Effectiveness**:

   Shielding effectiveness (SE) is a measure of how well a material or structure blocks RF signals. This is typically expressed in decibels (dB), where a higher SE indicates greater attenuation of RF signals. The SE of a material depends on several factors, including its thickness, conductivity, and the frequency range of the signals it is designed to block. A good shielding system will achieve high SE across a wide frequency spectrum.

3. **Continuous Coverage**:

   One of the challenges in designing an effective RF shielding system is ensuring that the entire area is adequately covered. RF waves can find their way through small gaps or holes, so it is important to design shielding systems that provide continuous coverage. This includes sealing seams, joints, and entry points, as well as ensuring that any cables, windows, or doors are also shielded.

4. **Grounding**:

    Proper grounding is essential for effective RF shielding. When an RF signal is blocked or absorbed by a shield, the absorbed energy must be safely dissipated to prevent it from reflecting or causing unwanted interference. Grounding helps direct this energy away from sensitive equipment and into the earth. A well-designed grounding system ensures that the shielding performs optimally and prevents any build-up of energy that could lead to signal degradation or safety risks.

5. **Compatibility with Existing Systems**:

    In many cases, anti-RF shielding must be integrated into existing systems. Whether retrofitting a building or adding shielding to a specific device, the design must take into account the constraints of the current environment, including space limitations, access to power sources, and the need to maintain system functionality without introducing new points of failure.

Types of Anti-RF Shielding

There are several types of anti-RF shielding that can be used depending on the application and environment. Each type has its unique strengths and considerations:

Faraday Cages

Applications

Conductive Coatings

Applications

Metal Enclosures and Shields

Applications

Gaskets and Seals

Applications

Flexible Shielding

Applications

Installation of Anti-RF Shielding

Once the design and materials have been chosen, the next step is to install the shielding system. Proper installation is critical to achieving the desired level of RF protection. Below are key considerations for the installation of anti-RF shielding:

1. **Site Survey and Planning**:

   A thorough site survey is the first step in the installation process. The survey should identify the sources of RF interference, the areas that need shielding, and the pathways that RF signals may use to penetrate the environment. The survey will also assess factors like building structure, power sources, ventilation, and existing communication systems to ensure compatibility with the shielding system.

2. **Installation of Materials**:

   Shielding materials must be carefully installed to ensure they provide continuous coverage. This includes applying conductive coatings, installing metal panels, and placing gaskets or seals at points where RF signals may enter or exit. The installation should ensure that no gaps remain where RF signals could leak through.

3. **Testing and Optimization**:

   After installation, it is essential to test the shielding system to ensure it meets the desired specifications. This typically involves measuring the signal strength inside and outside the shielded area to confirm that the RF signals have been adequately blocked. If necessary, adjustments or additional layers of shielding can be added to improve performance.

4. **Maintenance**:

    Like any other protective system, RF shielding requires periodic maintenance. This includes inspecting and repairing any physical damage to the shielding, ensuring that gaskets and seals remain intact, and conducting tests to verify the continued effectiveness of the system over time.

Challenges in Building and Installing Anti-RF Shielding

While anti-RF shielding is a highly effective method for controlling RF interference, the process of building and installing these systems is not without challenges. These include:

- **Cost**: High-quality shielding materials, such as metals and specialized coatings, can be expensive. Additionally, the installation process may require specialized labor and equipment, adding to the overall cost.
- **Complexity**: Designing a shielding system that provides comprehensive coverage across all frequencies and is effective in a given environment can be complex. Installation requires a high degree of precision to ensure that the system performs as intended.
- **Space Constraints**: In some cases, the space available for installation may be limited. Designing shielding solutions that are both effective and space-efficient is a critical consideration, particularly in commercial and residential applications.

Conclusion

Building and installing anti-RF shielding is an essential component in controlling RF interference and ensuring the integrity of sensitive electronic systems. By carefully selecting materials, designing the system, and ensuring proper installation and testing, organizations can protect their environments from the harmful effects of RF signals. As technology continues to advance, anti-RF shielding will remain an important tool for securing communication systems, protecting critical infrastructure, and maintaining operational performance across a wide range of industries.

In the next chapter, we will explore RF filtering and its role in managing and controlling RF signals in more detail. We will look at the different types of filters, their applications, and how to design and implement them for optimal performance.

Chapter 9: Overview of RF Filtering

In the world of radio frequency (RF) systems, filtering plays an essential role in ensuring that signals are transmitted and received with minimal interference. RF filtering involves using specific components and techniques to allow certain frequencies to pass through while blocking or attenuating others. Whether it's to prevent unwanted signals from interfering with sensitive communications or to ensure that only the desired signals are transmitted, RF filtering is a fundamental technology for maintaining the integrity of RF systems.

This chapter provides an overview of RF filtering, explaining the principles behind it, the different types of RF filters, and how they are used in various applications. Understanding the role of filters in managing RF signals will enable you to design more robust systems, reduce interference, and ensure optimal performance in a variety of environments.

What is RF Filtering?

RF filtering refers to the process of selectively passing or blocking certain frequencies of electromagnetic waves. It is used to control the spectrum of RF signals and prevent interference that could disrupt the performance of communication systems. Filters work by using electrical components, such as capacitors, inductors, and resistors, to create circuits that allow signals at specific frequencies to pass while rejecting others.

RF filters can be passive or active:

- **Passive filters** rely on components like resistors, inductors, and capacitors and do not require an external power source. They are commonly used in many RF applications due to their simplicity and reliability.
- **Active filters** include active components like transistors or operational amplifiers. They are used when more complex filtering is required, such as amplifying desired signals or achieving sharper cutoff frequencies.

The primary purpose of RF filtering is to eliminate unwanted signals, noise, or harmonics from a communication system, thereby improving signal quality and system performance.

The Role of RF Filters

RF filters serve several key functions in RF systems:

1. **Noise Reduction**: RF filters reduce the amount of noise that can be picked up by sensitive equipment. Unwanted signals from other devices, power lines, or environmental sources can degrade the quality of the desired signal. Filters block out these unwanted signals to improve signal clarity and quality.

2. **Frequency Separation**: Filters enable systems to operate on specific frequencies while avoiding interference from adjacent frequency bands. This is essential in environments where multiple communication systems share the same spectrum, such as in telecommunications, broadcasting, or military applications.

3. **Harmonic Suppression**: RF filters are used to prevent harmonics—unwanted frequencies generated by non-linear behavior in electronic components—from interfering with the primary signal. Harmonics can distort signals and cause inefficiencies in transmission.

4. **Signal Isolation**: RF filters can be used to isolate signals within a system, ensuring that signals from different devices or channels do not interfere with one another. This is especially important in systems that handle multiple communication channels, such as wireless networks and radio stations.

5. **Bandwidth Limiting**: Filters help limit the bandwidth of a signal to match the required specifications for communication. By restricting the range of frequencies that pass through, filters ensure that only the relevant signals are transmitted or received, improving the system's efficiency.

Types of RF Filters and Their Applications

There are several types of RF filters, each designed for different purposes based on the specific frequencies and signal characteristics involved. The four main types of RF filters are:

Low-Pass Filters (LPF)

Applications

High-Pass Filters (HPF)

Applications

Band-Pass Filters (BPF)

Applications

Band-Stop Filters (BSF)

Applications

Notch Filters

Applications

Designing and Implementing RF Filters

The design and implementation of RF filters depend on several factors, including the desired frequency range, the type of interference to be eliminated, and the characteristics of the system being protected. Below are some key considerations for designing and implementing effective RF filters:

1. **Cutoff Frequencies**: The cutoff frequency is the frequency at which a filter starts to attenuate the signal. For low-pass filters, this is the frequency above which the signal is attenuated, while for high-pass filters, it's the frequency below which the signal is blocked. Accurately determining the cutoff frequencies is crucial for effective filtering.
2. **Filter Order**: The order of a filter refers to the number of reactive components (such as inductors or capacitors) used to shape the frequency response. Higher-order filters provide steeper roll-offs, meaning they more sharply attenuate signals outside the desired frequency range. However, higher-order filters also introduce more complexity and may cause more signal distortion.
3. **Impedance Matching**: For filters to work effectively in an RF system, it is essential to ensure that the impedance of the filter matches the system's impedance. Mismatched impedance can lead to signal reflections, loss of power, and reduced filter performance.
4. **Power Handling**: RF filters must be designed to handle the power levels present in the system. Filters used in high-power systems, such as broadcasting or radar, require robust components capable of withstanding higher levels of RF power without damage.

5. **Size and Form Factor**: The physical size of the filter is another important consideration. In compact or portable devices, such as mobile phones or IoT devices, the filter must be small and lightweight while still providing the necessary filtering performance. Conversely, in large systems like radio towers or communication satellites, size may not be as constrained.

6. **Filter Materials**: The materials used in the construction of RF filters must be chosen based on their electrical properties. For instance, inductors with high Q-factor (quality factor) are used to create sharper filtering effects, while capacitors with stable dielectric properties are essential for maintaining filter performance across a broad range of frequencies.

Applications of RF Filters

RF filters are found in numerous applications across many industries. Some of the most notable include:

- **Telecommunications**: RF filters are used extensively in wireless communication systems to ensure that signals within specific frequency bands are transmitted and received without interference from adjacent bands. For example, filters in mobile phones and base stations help isolate channels in a crowded spectrum.
- **Broadcasting**: In television and radio broadcasting, RF filters help isolate signals within the allocated frequency bands and prevent interference from other transmitters.
- **Medical Equipment**: RF filters are critical in medical devices like MRI machines, pacemakers, and diagnostic equipment to ensure that they operate without interference from other nearby RF devices.
- **Military and Aerospace**: In military communications, radar systems, and avionics, RF filters help protect sensitive equipment from RF interference and ensure reliable performance in challenging environments.
- **Consumer Electronics**: RF filters are used in devices like televisions, Wi-Fi routers, and Bluetooth devices to ensure that they operate without interference from other devices.

Conclusion

RF filtering is a vital technique for controlling RF signals and preventing interference in communication systems. Filters allow only the desired signals to pass through, ensuring that systems operate efficiently and reliably. By understanding the principles behind RF filtering and the different types of filters available, you can design systems that effectively manage RF interference and ensure high-quality signal transmission.

In the next chapter, we will explore how RF filters can be designed and implemented to meet specific performance requirements, including the methods for measuring filter performance and ensuring that filters are properly integrated into RF systems.

Chapter 10: Designing and Implementing RF Filters

In the previous chapter, we examined the different types of RF filters and their essential functions in maintaining signal integrity and preventing interference. In this chapter, we will dive deeper into the practical aspects of designing and implementing RF filters. This process involves understanding the system requirements, selecting the appropriate filter type, optimizing performance, and integrating the filter into a broader RF environment.

Effective filter design is crucial in applications ranging from consumer electronics to critical military communications. A well-designed filter can drastically improve system performance, whereas a poorly designed filter may cause more harm than good, introducing unwanted losses or distortion.

This chapter will walk through the steps and considerations involved in designing and implementing RF filters, from the theoretical groundwork to real-world applications. It will also cover the key metrics and methodologies used to evaluate the performance of RF filters.

1. Understanding the Design Process for RF Filters

Designing an RF filter involves a balance of theory, practical considerations, and system constraints. The goal is to meet specific performance criteria while ensuring that the filter fits seamlessly into the larger RF system. Below are the essential steps in designing an RF filter:

1.1. Define the Filter's Purpose

The first step in any filter design is defining its purpose within the system. What problem is the filter intended to solve? Is it filtering out unwanted harmonics, blocking noise from other frequencies, or isolating specific signal bands? The filter's purpose will directly influence the type of filter chosen and its specific parameters.

Common design goals include:

- Attenuating undesired frequencies (such as interference or harmonics)
- Isolating signal bands (band-pass or band-stop)
- Providing adequate attenuation without significant signal distortion or loss
- Minimizing insertion loss (the loss of signal power as it passes through the filter)
- Matching the impedance of the filter to the surrounding system to prevent reflections

1.2. Determine the Cutoff Frequencies

The cutoff frequency is a critical design parameter in RF filters. For low-pass filters, this is the frequency beyond which all signals are attenuated, while for high-pass filters, it is the frequency below which signals are blocked. For band-pass filters, the cutoff frequencies define the range of frequencies that can pass through.

The performance of the filter depends heavily on the precise selection of cutoff frequencies, and the "sharpness" of the filter's transition from passband to stopband. The goal is to balance performance with practicality:

- Sharp cutoff: Higher-order filters (with more components) can achieve steeper roll-offs, but this introduces more complexity.
- Gentle cutoff: Simpler filters with less steep roll-offs may be easier to implement but might not be as effective in rejecting unwanted frequencies.

1.3. Choose the Filter Topology

There are several standard filter topologies used in RF design, and the choice of topology affects the filter's performance, complexity, and implementation.

- **Butterworth Filter**: Known for its maximally flat frequency response in the passband, it provides a good balance of performance and ease of design. It is commonly used when flatness is a priority.
- **Chebyshev Filter**: This type has a steeper roll-off compared to the Butterworth filter but introduces ripples in the passband. It is ideal when a sharp transition is needed.
- **Elliptic Filter**: Also known as a Zolotarev filter, it provides the steepest roll-off of all, with ripples in both the passband and the stopband. It's used in situations where a very sharp transition is essential.
- **Bessel Filter**: Known for maintaining a linear phase response, Bessel filters are preferred in applications where signal phase preservation is more important than frequency response.
- **Cauer Filter (Ladder Filter)**: This filter type is particularly useful for low-frequency applications and provides a good compromise between performance and complexity.

1.4. Select Filter Components

Once the filter topology is decided, the next step is selecting the components that will make up the filter. The most common components used in RF filters are:

- **Inductors**: Inductors are used in filters for their ability to store and release energy in magnetic fields. They are essential for creating reactive elements in the filter circuit.
- **Capacitors**: Capacitors store energy in electric fields and are used to block DC signals while passing AC signals. In RF filters, capacitors control the frequency response.
- **Resistors**: Resistors are used to control the damping and overall Q-factor of the filter, influencing the sharpness of the frequency response.

For filters used in high-frequency systems, components with low parasitic capacitance and inductance are essential for maintaining the integrity of the filter design.

2. Implementing the RF Filter

Implementing an RF filter in an actual system involves not only designing the filter circuit but also integrating it into the larger system. The following steps are essential when implementing a filter:

2.1. Impedance Matching

One of the most critical aspects of filter implementation is ensuring proper impedance matching. If the filter's impedance does not match the impedance of the system (usually 50 ohms for RF systems), signal reflections can occur, which can cause signal degradation, standing waves, and reduced system performance.

Impedance matching can be achieved through various techniques, including:

- **Transmission line matching**: Use of transmission lines (like coaxial cables or microstrip lines) to match the impedance of the filter to that of the system.
- **Balun transformers**: These can help match impedance between unbalanced and balanced systems, such as in antenna systems.

2.2. Physical Layout and Miniaturization

Filters often need to be miniaturized for integration into compact electronic devices. Designers need to account for the size, shape, and positioning of components within the available space. This includes:

- **Surface-mount components**: For compact devices, surface-mount inductors and capacitors are often used.
- **Multi-layer PCBs**: Multiple layers can be used to route signals through various components without excessive space.
- **Shielding and grounding**: Proper grounding and shielding are necessary to avoid external interference and signal leakage.

2.3. Prototype Testing

Once the filter is designed and physically constructed, it is essential to test its performance. Key tests include:

- **Frequency response testing**: Ensuring the filter achieves the desired cutoff frequencies and attenuation levels.
- **Insertion loss measurement**: Determining the amount of signal loss as it passes through the filter.
- **Return loss testing**: Verifying that the filter matches the system's impedance and minimizes reflections.

Prototyping also involves testing the filter in various operating conditions to ensure robustness under different frequencies, temperatures, and environmental conditions.

2.4. Integration into Larger Systems

Once the filter is tested and optimized, it must be integrated into the broader RF system. This involves:

- **System calibration**: The system must be calibrated to account for any phase or amplitude changes introduced by the filter.
- **Signal routing**: Ensure that the filter is placed in the right part of the system to effectively block or pass the desired frequencies. Filters can be integrated at various stages in an RF system, including between signal sources and amplifiers or between amplifiers and antennas.

3. Evaluating Filter Performance

To ensure that a filter is performing as expected, several key metrics are used to assess its behavior:

3.1. Insertion Loss

Insertion loss refers to the amount of signal power lost as it passes through the filter. The lower the insertion loss, the better the filter allows the desired signal to pass. Insertion loss is critical in high-frequency applications, where even small losses can degrade signal quality.

3.2. Attenuation

Attenuation is the reduction in signal strength at frequencies outside the passband. Effective filters provide high attenuation in the stopband, ensuring that unwanted signals are blocked efficiently.

3.3. Bandwidth

Bandwidth refers to the frequency range over which the filter allows signals to pass with minimal attenuation. For band-pass filters, the bandwidth must be carefully tuned to ensure that it encompasses the entire desired signal spectrum.

3.4. Phase Shift

Filters can introduce phase shifts in the signal, especially when they have a non-linear phase response. Phase shifts can be problematic in systems that require precise timing, such as data transmission or radar systems. Filters with a linear phase response, such as Bessel filters, minimize these issues.

4. Conclusion

Designing and implementing RF filters is a crucial part of managing radio frequency signals in modern communication systems. A well-designed filter can improve performance by reducing noise, isolating channels, and enhancing signal integrity. Understanding the principles behind filter design, from selecting the right filter type to evaluating performance metrics, is essential for building efficient and reliable RF systems.

In the next chapter, we will focus on measuring the performance of RF systems, including how to assess the effectiveness of filters and other components in real-world environments.

Chapter 11: Measuring RF Signal and Filter Performance

In the previous chapters, we've explored the theory, design, and implementation of various RF shielding, absorption, and filtering techniques. Now, it's time to discuss how to evaluate and measure the effectiveness of these systems. Accurate measurement of RF signals and the performance of RF filters is essential to ensure that a designed solution performs as expected and meets the required specifications.

In this chapter, we will focus on the key methods and tools used to measure RF signals, analyze their quality, and assess the effectiveness of RF filters. Understanding how to interpret these measurements will enable engineers and technicians to optimize RF systems, troubleshoot performance issues, and validate that the design goals have been achieved.

1. The Importance of RF Signal Measurement

Accurate measurement of RF signals is critical for verifying the behavior of a radio frequency system. Whether you are designing a new system, maintaining an existing one, or troubleshooting an issue, precise measurements provide insights into signal strength, frequency response, phase, and noise levels. These measurements are the foundation for ensuring that the RF components — including filters, absorbers, and anti-RF devices — perform their intended functions.

Key aspects of RF signal measurement include:

- **Signal Strength**: The power level of the RF signal is a critical metric. In communication systems, weak signals can result in poor data transmission quality, while overly strong signals may cause distortion or interference.
- **Signal Frequency**: Ensuring that a signal operates within the correct frequency range is essential for proper system performance. Frequency is the primary factor that filters target, either passing or blocking certain bands.
- **Phase**: The phase of the signal is particularly important in systems where timing and synchronization are critical, such as in radar or high-speed communication systems.
- **Signal Integrity**: Signal integrity encompasses multiple factors, including waveform distortion, noise, and other impairments that affect the overall quality of the signal.

2. RF Measurement Tools and Techniques

Several tools and techniques are available to measure RF signals and analyze the performance of RF filters. Each tool has specific strengths depending on the measurement goals, frequency range, and system setup.

2.1. Spectrum Analyzers

A spectrum analyzer is one of the most essential tools for measuring RF signals. It provides a graphical representation of the frequency spectrum, allowing you to observe the power of signals over a range of frequencies.

Key uses of spectrum analyzers:

- **Measuring signal power**: Spectrum analyzers show how much power is present at different frequencies, allowing you to evaluate signal strength and identify spurious emissions or harmonics.
- **Identifying interference**: They can detect unwanted signals, noise, or interference that may impact system performance.
- **Analyzing frequency response**: Spectrum analyzers can help you verify whether a filter is allowing the correct frequencies to pass while attenuating others.

When using a spectrum analyzer, important parameters to consider include:

- **Frequency span**: The range of frequencies displayed.
- **Resolution bandwidth (RBW)**: This controls the analyzer's ability to resolve closely spaced signals. A narrow RBW allows better resolution, but takes more time to analyze.
- **Average or peak hold**: The display mode to observe the average behavior or peak levels of signals over time.

2.2. Vector Network Analyzers (VNA)

A Vector Network Analyzer (VNA) is used to measure the complex transmission and reflection characteristics of RF components. This tool is particularly useful when analyzing filters, amplifiers, antennas, and other components that affect the flow of RF signals.

VNAs measure parameters such as:

S-parameters (scattering parameters)

- **Measuring insertion loss**: The reduction in signal strength as it passes through a component or system.
- **Measuring return loss**: The amount of reflected signal that results from impedance mismatches.

VNAs are indispensable for:

- **Testing filters**: VNAs can show the frequency response of a filter, illustrating the attenuation in the stopband and the bandwidth in the passband.
- **Characterizing phase shift**: VNAs provide phase information that is crucial for applications where phase integrity is important.

2.3. Power Meters

Power meters measure the absolute power level of an RF signal, typically in watts or dBm (decibels relative to one milliwatt). They are essential for determining the overall strength of the signal, including both transmitted and received power.

Power meters are important for:

- **Measuring transmitted power**: Ensuring that the signal being sent out is at the appropriate power level for the application.
- **Detecting signal loss**: Measuring the power of a signal after it has passed through a filter or other component can show how much power is lost.
- **Verifying system performance**: Power meters help verify that the power levels are within the acceptable range for a given system or application.

2.4. Time Domain Reflectometer (TDR)

A Time Domain Reflectometer is a specialized tool used for diagnosing impedance mismatches in RF systems. It works by sending a signal through the system and measuring the reflected signal to determine the location and magnitude of impedance mismatches.

Key applications of TDR:

- **Locating cable faults**: TDRs are effective at detecting issues in coaxial cables or connectors that may affect RF performance.
- **Assessing impedance matching**: Ensuring that components, such as filters and antennas, are properly matched to the system's impedance to minimize reflections.

2.5. Signal Generators

A signal generator is used to create RF signals with specific frequencies and power levels for testing. Signal generators are useful for:

- **Testing filters**: By generating a test signal with known parameters, you can evaluate how well a filter attenuates or passes specific frequencies.
- **Simulating real-world signals**: Signal generators can simulate interference, allowing you to test how well RF systems handle unwanted signals or noise.

3. Key Performance Metrics for RF Filters

Once you have the right measurement tools in place, it's important to evaluate the performance of RF filters against certain key metrics. These metrics will help you determine whether the filter is functioning as expected and meeting design goals.

3.1. Insertion Loss

Insertion loss refers to the reduction in signal strength as the signal passes through the filter. It is often measured in dB and represents the amount of attenuation experienced by the signal. A good filter will have low insertion loss in the passband.

To measure insertion loss:

- Use a network analyzer to measure the signal strength before and after the filter.
- Compare the output power to the input power, and calculate the loss.

3.2. Attenuation Characteristics

Attenuation is the reduction in the signal strength in the stopband. A filter should attenuate signals outside the desired passband as much as possible. The sharper the transition between the passband and stopband, the better the filter's performance.

To evaluate attenuation:

- Use a spectrum analyzer or VNA to examine the signal in the stopband.
- Measure the level of the signal outside the passband and compare it to the level in the passband.

3.3. Bandwidth

Bandwidth refers to the range of frequencies that the filter allows to pass with minimal attenuation. A good band-pass filter will have a defined bandwidth with minimal signal loss. For low-pass and high-pass filters, bandwidth is also important in determining the cutoff point.

To measure bandwidth:

Use a spectrum analyzer to observe the signal and determine the frequencies where the signal drops below the specified threshold.

3.4. Phase Response

In certain applications, such as communications and radar, phase response is critical. Filters with linear phase response are often preferred because they preserve the integrity of the signal's waveform and prevent distortion.

To measure phase response:

- Use a VNA to observe the phase shift as the signal passes through the filter.
- Ensure that the filter introduces minimal phase distortion across the passband.

4. Conclusion

Measuring the performance of RF signals and filters is crucial to ensure that RF systems operate efficiently and meet design specifications. By using the appropriate tools, such as spectrum analyzers, VNAs, and power meters, engineers can verify that RF components are functioning as expected. Key performance metrics like insertion loss, attenuation, bandwidth, and phase response are essential for evaluating filter performance.

In the next chapter, we will discuss the concept of white noise and its critical role in RF systems, particularly in mitigating interference and enhancing security.

Chapter 12: Introduction to White Noise

In the realm of RF technologies, understanding and managing noise is essential. While much of the focus is often on the transmission and reception of useful signals, noise—particularly white noise—plays a significant role in shaping the performance of RF systems. This chapter introduces the concept of white noise, its physical properties, and its applications in RF interference, security systems, and beyond.

1. What is White Noise?

White noise, in the context of RF and signal processing, refers to a type of noise that contains a wide range of frequencies, all of which are present at roughly equal intensities. The name "white" comes from its analogy to white light, which contains all visible colors. In the same way, white noise encompasses all frequencies within a given range, with a flat spectral density, meaning that no particular frequency is more dominant than any other.

White noise is often considered to have the following properties:

- **Uniform Power Across Frequencies**: White noise has a flat power spectral density, meaning that its power is distributed equally across the frequency spectrum.
- **Randomness**: White noise is random in nature, with unpredictable fluctuations in amplitude over time, which makes it an important factor to consider when designing communication systems.
- **Gaussian Distribution**: In many cases, white noise is assumed to have a Gaussian distribution of amplitudes. This makes its statistical properties predictable and easy to model for various applications.

2. The Physics of White Noise

From a physical standpoint, white noise is generated by the random movement of particles (such as electrons) within a system. In electronic circuits, thermal noise (also known as Johnson-Nyquist noise) is a type of white noise that arises due to the random thermal motion of charge carriers inside resistive elements.

White noise is characterized by:

- **Infinite Bandwidth**: In theory, white noise extends infinitely in both the low and high-frequency directions. In practice, the bandwidth of white noise is constrained by the system's frequency range or the bandwidth limitations of the equipment used to generate or measure it.
- **Constant Power Spectral Density**: The power spectral density remains constant over frequency, meaning that energy is spread uniformly across the frequency spectrum, as opposed to other types of noise like pink noise, which has more power in lower frequencies.

While white noise is often modeled as a continuous signal, real-world systems may have limitations that restrict the frequencies and amplitudes of the noise. Still, the concept of white noise remains central to understanding how various types of interference affect RF systems.

3. Sources of White Noise in RF Systems

White noise can be generated by various sources in RF systems, and it can appear in both the transmission and reception processes. Some common sources include:

- **Thermal Noise**: Also known as Johnson-Nyquist noise, this is caused by the random motion of electrons in conductors due to thermal energy. Thermal noise is ubiquitous and can be found in virtually all electronic devices, from resistors to semiconductors.
- **Shot Noise**: Arising from the discrete nature of electric charge, shot noise occurs due to the random arrival of charge carriers (such as electrons) at a junction or during the flow of current.
- **Flicker Noise**: While technically not white noise, flicker noise (or 1/f noise) is often present in RF systems and can combine with white noise to impact the overall noise performance. It tends to dominate at lower frequencies.
- **Atmospheric Noise**: White noise can also be caused by various environmental factors, such as electrical discharges in the atmosphere, lightning, or solar activity.

The interaction of white noise with other signals is a crucial aspect to understand when designing RF systems. It can degrade the quality of communication channels, introduce errors, and reduce the efficiency of signal processing techniques.

4. Using White Noise for RF Interference

White noise is not always an unwanted phenomenon. It can be intentionally used to test, disrupt, or mask RF signals, depending on the application. In some contexts, its ability to occupy the entire frequency spectrum makes it useful as a form of jamming or interference.

4.1. RF Jamming

White noise can be used as an effective method for jamming RF communications. By broadcasting white noise across a wide frequency range, an adversary can overwhelm a targeted RF system, effectively blocking communications and preventing the reception of valid signals. This method is often employed in military and security applications where communication systems need to be protected from interception or tampering.

While using white noise for jamming is effective, it must be carefully managed:

- **Power Control**: The intensity of the white noise signal must be carefully calibrated. Too much power could disrupt not only the targeted system but also other nearby systems, potentially causing unintended collateral effects.
- **Bandwidth**: The white noise signal must cover the frequency band used by the target system. This requires accurate knowledge of the target system's operating frequencies to ensure the noise is effective.

4.2. Signal Masking

On the other hand, white noise is also used for masking other signals, especially in environments where communication security is critical. By embedding white noise into a signal or broadcast, it becomes harder for unauthorized parties to extract meaningful information from the transmission. This is useful in situations where confidentiality is essential, such as military operations, secure communications, or private data transmission.

Signal masking with white noise is typically used in conjunction with encryption or other security methods to make the signal harder to intercept and decipher. While white noise can obscure the signal, additional cryptographic methods are often needed to provide robust security.

5. The Role of White Noise in Security Systems

White noise plays a critical role in enhancing security in various RF systems, particularly in environments where protection against eavesdropping or unauthorized monitoring is a concern.

5.1. RF Stealth Technology

White noise is often incorporated into RF stealth technology to reduce the detectability of systems. By using a broad spectrum of white noise, stealth systems can blend their emissions with background noise, making it more difficult for adversaries to detect or track their signals. This is particularly relevant in military applications where radar and communication systems need to evade detection.

5.2. Secure Communication Channels

In secure communication systems, white noise is employed as part of frequency-hopping or spread-spectrum techniques. These methods spread the signal over a broad frequency band, reducing the likelihood of interception by unauthorized listeners. White noise can be used to mask the signal, further obfuscating its presence and making it harder to detect or decrypt.

5.3. Noise-Based Security Protocols

Another innovative use of white noise is in noise-based security protocols. These systems employ white noise to scramble or randomize the transmission of critical data, ensuring that even if the data is intercepted, it is rendered meaningless without the correct decryption method or key.

6. White Noise in RF Shielding

White noise can also be integrated into RF shielding systems as a countermeasure to prevent external signals from affecting sensitive electronics. In RF shielding, white noise may be used to create a "masking" layer around electronic devices or systems. By introducing a controlled level of white noise within a shielded environment, any unwanted signals that attempt to penetrate the shield can be effectively masked by the noise.

For example, in highly sensitive environments like research laboratories or secure communication centers, introducing white noise can help ensure that the devices within the shielded area are not affected by external RF interference. This can enhance the overall performance and reliability of the system.

7. Conclusion

White noise plays a multifaceted role in the world of RF systems, with applications ranging from interference and jamming to security enhancement and signal masking. Its ability to occupy a wide frequency range makes it both a potential threat and a valuable tool in RF design. By understanding the physics and applications of white noise, engineers can leverage it to optimize RF systems for security, reliability, and performance.

In the following chapters, we will dive deeper into the use of white noise in specific RF applications, including its role in military operations, consumer electronics, and the emerging field of 5G technologies. Understanding how to control and manipulate white noise will be a key factor in mastering RF technology and ensuring the success of modern RF systems.

Chapter 13: RF Blocking in Military and Security Applications

RF blocking plays a pivotal role in military and security applications where the need for secure communications and protection against interception is critical. This chapter explores the strategies, technologies, and considerations involved in RF blocking within defense and security sectors, highlighting its importance for national security, intelligence, and covert operations.

1. The Need for RF Blocking in Military and Security

In military and security environments, RF signals are often the primary means of communication and data exchange. These signals, however, are highly susceptible to interception, jamming, and other forms of disruption by adversaries. RF blocking is crucial for maintaining the integrity of communication systems, ensuring that sensitive information does not fall into the wrong hands. It serves several key purposes:

- **Confidentiality**: Preventing unauthorized interception of military communications, preventing adversaries from eavesdropping on strategic plans or tactical movements.
- **Counteracting Jamming**: Protecting communication channels from adversaries who use jamming techniques to disrupt the flow of information.
- **Signal Denial**: Ensuring that the enemy cannot detect or track the position or activity of military units through RF emissions.
- **Operational Integrity**: Safeguarding the functionality of secure systems against external RF interference, ensuring that critical missions are not compromised.

RF blocking is not merely a reactive measure to prevent eavesdropping but also a proactive strategy to deter threats and ensure the operational success of missions, from battlefield communications to covert intelligence gathering.

2. RF Shielding and Stealth Technology

Military and security organizations have long relied on RF shielding to block unwanted signals and to ensure the security of their operations. RF shielding involves the use of materials, designs, and strategies to protect electronic devices and communication systems from external RF interference and to prevent the leakage of sensitive signals that could be intercepted.

2.1. Types of RF Shielding Materials for Military Applications

Military-grade RF shielding materials are carefully chosen for their effectiveness in blocking a wide range of frequencies. Some common materials include:

- **Metals (Copper, Aluminum, Steel)**: Metals are highly conductive and effective in reflecting or absorbing RF signals. Copper and aluminum are particularly popular due to their high conductivity and ease of application.
- **Conductive Coatings and Films**: Thin, flexible conductive materials can be applied to various surfaces to provide lightweight, effective shielding without adding significant bulk.
- **Carbon-based Materials**: These include materials such as carbon nanotubes and graphene, which have excellent electrical conductivity and can be used in advanced shielding applications.
- **Ferrites**: Magnetic materials, such as ferrites, are used to absorb high-frequency signals, making them effective in protecting sensitive electronic equipment from RF interference.

2.2. Electromagnetic Shielding Enclosures

For protecting critical communication systems and electronic devices, military applications often employ electromagnetic shielding enclosures. These enclosures are designed to completely surround sensitive equipment with shielding materials, creating a Faraday cage effect that prevents both incoming and outgoing RF signals from escaping or entering. This is particularly important in covert operations where maintaining the secrecy of electronic devices is paramount.

Examples of RF shielding enclosures include:

- **Portable Shielded Rooms**: These are mobile, temporary enclosures that can be set up in the field to protect communication devices from interception or interference.
- **Vehicle Shielding**: Military vehicles and equipment often require custom shielding solutions to prevent RF leakage from onboard communication systems. This ensures that the vehicle's location and movements cannot be tracked through RF signals.
- **Antenna Shielding**: Specialized shielding for antennas can be used to protect both transmitting and receiving equipment, ensuring that the signal remains secure.

3. RF Jamming and Anti-Jamming Techniques

In military operations, one of the most important concerns is ensuring that RF signals are not vulnerable to interference or jamming. RF jamming is a method used by adversaries to intentionally disrupt the communication channels of military units by emitting powerful RF signals on the same frequencies. This prevents legitimate communication, leading to confusion and vulnerability.

3.1. Types of RF Jamming

- **Spot Jamming**: Involves transmitting a continuous wave of noise or interference on a specific frequency band to block communication.
- **Sweep Jamming**: Involves transmitting jamming signals across a range of frequencies, making it difficult to establish a clear communication channel.
- **Barrage Jamming**: A more aggressive form of jamming that floods a wide frequency spectrum with interference, rendering it almost impossible to transmit or receive any communication.

3.2. Anti-Jamming Techniques

To counter RF jamming, military and security organizations use various anti-jamming techniques, including:

- **Frequency Hopping Spread Spectrum (FHSS)**: This technique involves rapidly changing the frequency of a communication signal to avoid jamming. By constantly switching between frequencies in a pseudo-random sequence, a signal becomes harder to intercept or disrupt.
- **Direct Sequence Spread Spectrum (DSSS)**: DSSS spreads the signal over a wide bandwidth by multiplying the signal with a high-rate data stream, making it more resistant to jamming.
- **Adaptive Power Control**: This involves adjusting the transmission power of the RF signal to ensure that it remains strong enough to be received clearly even in the presence of jamming.
- **Jammer Detection and Localization**: By using specialized sensors and algorithms, military units can detect the presence of jamming signals and locate the source, allowing for targeted countermeasures.

3.3. Anti-Jamming in Communications Systems

To maintain the integrity of military communications, advanced systems are designed to automatically detect and avoid interference. These systems use various techniques, such as:

- **Error Correction Codes**: These codes help to recover lost or corrupted data due to interference, ensuring that critical messages are transmitted without errors.
- **Cross-Platform Communication**: Redundant communication channels, including satellite, radio, and secure internet protocols, allow for the continuous exchange of information, even when one channel is disrupted.

4. RF Blocking in Security Systems

Beyond military applications, RF blocking also plays a crucial role in enhancing the security of other high-risk environments, such as:

- **Critical Infrastructure**: Protecting power grids, water treatment plants, and other essential services from cyber-attacks or RF-based interference.
- **Prison Security**: RF-blocking technology is used to prevent inmates from using smuggled mobile phones or unauthorized communication devices to contact the outside world.
- **Secure Government Facilities**: Ensuring that sensitive government offices, data centers, and embassies remain protected from eavesdropping and hacking attempts that rely on RF communication.

4.1. Implementing RF Blocking in Security Systems

RF blocking in security systems typically involves the installation of Faraday cages, jamming-resistant communication equipment, and the use of advanced encryption techniques to protect signals. In high-security areas, RF surveillance tools are also deployed to monitor and detect unauthorized RF activity.

- **Integrated RF Blocking Systems**: These systems can automatically detect unauthorized RF signals and activate countermeasures to disrupt or block them. Such systems are often used in sensitive military installations, secure government buildings, and critical infrastructure sites.
- **Mobile RF Blocking Systems**: Mobile jamming and RF blocking units can be deployed to secure areas or to neutralize threats during operations. These systems are often portable, flexible, and can be rapidly set up and dismantled.

5. Future Trends in RF Blocking for Military and Security

As technology evolves, so too do the threats and challenges related to RF communications. The future of RF blocking in military and security applications will be shaped by several key trends:

- **Integration with Cybersecurity**: RF blocking systems will increasingly integrate with broader cybersecurity strategies to create multi-layered defense mechanisms against both RF-based and digital threats.
- **AI-Driven Detection**: Machine learning and AI will play an increasing role in identifying patterns of RF interference, jamming attempts, and unauthorized communication. These technologies will be capable of automatically adapting and responding to new threats in real-time.
- **Quantum Communication**: Quantum encryption and communication systems promise to revolutionize RF security by providing communication channels that are fundamentally immune to interception or hacking, making traditional RF blocking methods even more effective.

6. Conclusion

RF blocking is a cornerstone of modern military and security operations. Whether it involves shielding sensitive communication systems from unwanted interference, preventing jamming, or securing confidential communications, the ability to control and block RF signals is critical for ensuring national security, operational success, and the safety of military personnel. As RF technologies continue to evolve, so too will the methods and tools used to counteract threats and enhance security. Understanding and implementing effective RF blocking strategies will remain a vital aspect of protecting both military assets and civilian infrastructure from interference and malicious RF-based attacks.

Chapter 14: RF Shielding in Consumer Electronics

RF shielding plays a crucial role in the design and operation of modern consumer electronics, from smartphones and laptops to home appliances and wearable devices. As technology continues to advance and the demand for wireless communication increases, ensuring that devices function optimally without interference from or contributing to RF pollution becomes increasingly important. This chapter explores the principles and practices of RF shielding in consumer electronics, focusing on its applications, design considerations, and the evolving regulatory landscape.

1. The Growing Need for RF Shielding in Consumer Electronics

Consumer electronics are part of an increasingly interconnected ecosystem where devices communicate over various wireless networks, including Wi-Fi, Bluetooth, NFC, and cellular connections. This widespread use of RF signals, while beneficial for convenience and performance, brings with it a number of challenges related to interference, signal degradation, and exposure to potentially harmful radiation. As consumer electronics become more compact and powerful, the need for effective RF shielding becomes essential to ensure:

- **Signal Integrity**: Maintaining the quality of communication signals to ensure that devices can perform as intended without interference.
- **Minimizing Interference**: Preventing RF emissions from one device from interfering with the performance of nearby devices, ensuring that all devices in an environment operate smoothly.
- **Electromagnetic Compatibility (EMC)**: Ensuring that devices comply with electromagnetic compatibility standards, preventing excessive RF emissions that could affect other electronic devices or interfere with communication systems.
- **Radiation Safety**: Reducing human exposure to electromagnetic radiation, particularly in the case of portable devices such as mobile phones and wearable electronics.

RF shielding in consumer electronics is not only about protecting devices from external RF interference but also about minimizing the unintentional radiation emitted by the device itself, which could negatively affect the surrounding environment or its users.

2. Principles of RF Shielding in Consumer Electronics

The goal of RF shielding in consumer electronics is to ensure that electronic components function optimally while preventing unwanted RF signals from either entering or leaving the device. The effectiveness of shielding depends on several key principles:

Material Selection

- **Conductivity**: High conductivity is essential for reflecting and absorbing RF signals. Metals like copper and aluminum are particularly effective in shielding because they can reflect RF signals effectively.
- **Thickness**: The thickness of the shielding material determines how well it can attenuate electromagnetic waves. A thicker material generally provides better attenuation, but it must be balanced with the weight and size constraints of the device.
- **Porosity**: In some cases, materials with low porosity are used to reduce RF leakage, ensuring that the shield forms a more continuous barrier.

Design Considerations

- **Enclosures**: Devices often employ metal or conductive plastic enclosures to act as Faraday cages, blocking RF signals from entering or exiting the device. The design must ensure that the entire device is shielded, with careful attention to any gaps or openings that could allow RF leakage.
- **Shielded Compartments**: In more complex devices, such as smartphones or laptops, certain components (e.g., processors, radios) may require localized shielding to prevent interference between sensitive components and to shield RF emissions.

Antenna Placement and Shielding

3. Types of RF Shielding in Consumer Electronics

Several types of RF shielding solutions are used in consumer electronics to achieve the desired level of protection against electromagnetic interference (EMI) and to ensure that devices meet industry standards for EMC. These solutions are selected based on the specific requirements of the device, its operating environment, and the types of interference it is expected to encounter.

3.1. Metal Shielding

Metal shielding remains the most widely used method of RF shielding in consumer electronics. Metals are effective at both blocking and reflecting electromagnetic waves. The most commonly used metals in RF shielding include:

- **Aluminum**: Lightweight and cost-effective, aluminum is widely used for shielding enclosures in consumer electronics. Its good conductivity makes it effective at blocking both low- and high-frequency RF signals.
- **Copper**: Copper is an excellent conductor and is often used in higher-end applications where superior shielding is required. Copper's high conductivity makes it particularly effective at attenuating a wide range of RF frequencies.
- **Steel**: Steel is often used for structural components that require both shielding and mechanical strength. It is typically more durable than aluminum or copper but heavier and more expensive.

3.2. Conductive Coatings

Conductive coatings are applied to the surface of non-metallic materials to provide a lightweight alternative to metal shielding. These coatings are typically made of conductive materials such as:

- **Conductive Paint**: This is a form of paint that contains metallic particles, such as silver or copper, which provide the necessary conductivity to shield RF signals. Conductive paint is often used in smaller or more compact devices where space is limited.
- **Conductive Films**: Thin layers of conductive material that can be applied to the inside of enclosures or directly onto circuit boards. These films are ideal for situations where traditional metal shielding is impractical.

3.3. Conductive Plastics

Some consumer electronic devices, particularly those designed for portability, utilize conductive plastics. These materials offer the dual benefits of being lightweight and providing adequate RF shielding without the bulk and weight of metals. Conductive plastics are increasingly used in the construction of enclosures for devices like smartphones, tablets, and wearables.

4. Shielding for Specific Consumer Electronics

Different types of consumer electronics have unique RF shielding needs based on their functions, operating environments, and regulatory standards.

4.1. Smartphones and Mobile Devices

Smartphones are perhaps the most RF-sensitive consumer electronics, as they rely on multiple wireless technologies (Wi-Fi, Bluetooth, cellular, NFC) while also being highly compact. Shielding must balance signal strength and interference protection, making careful antenna placement and effective internal shielding essential.

- **Shielded Compartments**: Smartphones often have internal compartments dedicated to shielding sensitive components, such as the display, battery, and antennas. These compartments prevent interference from RF signals generated by other components.
- **RF Absorbing Materials**: To minimize electromagnetic radiation from antennas, RF-absorbing materials are often used to prevent unwanted emissions.

4.2. Wearable Devices

Wearables, such as smartwatches and fitness trackers, are also subject to RF interference concerns, particularly because they are worn close to the body. Shielding must ensure that both communication signals (e.g., Bluetooth) and the device's own RF emissions do not interfere with other electronics or cause health concerns.

4.3. Laptops and Personal Computers

Laptops and desktop computers use various wireless technologies, including Wi-Fi, Bluetooth, and cellular connections. The shielding in these devices is usually integrated into the chassis or as specific enclosures for wireless modules. Shielding is critical to maintaining data integrity and preventing unwanted interference with other nearby devices, especially in crowded environments such as offices.

5. Regulatory and Industry Standards

As RF shielding becomes more important in consumer electronics, industry standards and regulations play an essential role in ensuring devices meet the necessary electromagnetic compatibility (EMC) guidelines. These standards, set by bodies such as the **Federal Communications Commission (FCC)** in the U.S., the **European Telecommunications Standards Institute (ETSI)** in Europe, and the **International Electrotechnical Commission (IEC)** globally, help govern the acceptable levels of RF emissions and the shielding required for devices.

Devices that do not comply with these standards may experience performance degradation or interference with other devices. In many cases, the manufacturer must prove compliance through testing and certification before the product can be sold in regulated markets.

6. The Future of RF Shielding in Consumer Electronics

As consumer electronics continue to evolve, the demands for more effective RF shielding solutions will increase. Future trends include:

- **Miniaturization**: As devices become smaller and more compact, the need for more efficient, lightweight shielding solutions will grow.
- **Smart Materials**: The development of smart, adaptive materials that can dynamically change their shielding properties in response to external RF environments will offer new opportunities for enhanced device performance and reduced interference.
- **5G and Beyond**: With the advent of 5G technology and future wireless networks, RF shielding will need to evolve to accommodate higher frequencies and greater data throughput while ensuring minimal interference between devices.

7. Conclusion

RF shielding in consumer electronics is critical to ensuring the performance, reliability, and safety of modern devices. As wireless communication becomes more ubiquitous and devices become increasingly interconnected, effective RF shielding will continue to be a key element in the design of consumer electronics. By understanding the principles of shielding, selecting appropriate materials, and staying informed about industry regulations, manufacturers can ensure that their products meet the needs of consumers while minimizing interference and exposure to harmful RF radiation. The future of RF shielding holds exciting possibilities, driven by advancements in materials science and the growing demand for smarter, more efficient electronic devices.

Chapter 15: Challenges and Troubleshooting in RF Shielding

In the field of RF shielding, practitioners often encounter a range of challenges, whether they are designing a shielding system for a sensitive military application or a consumer electronic device. Successfully addressing these issues requires a deep understanding of the physics of electromagnetic interference (EMI), as well as an ability to apply various shielding techniques. In this chapter, we will explore some of the common challenges faced in RF shielding projects and provide strategies for troubleshooting and overcoming these difficulties. This chapter also underscores the importance of an iterative and methodical approach to solving RF-related problems.

1. Understanding the Key Challenges in RF Shielding

RF shielding, while effective in many applications, is not without its challenges. Some of the key hurdles include:

1.1. Inadequate Shielding Effectiveness

One of the most common problems in RF shielding is insufficient attenuation of electromagnetic signals. This can occur for several reasons, including:

- **Material Choice**: The shielding material may not have the required conductivity or thickness to effectively block or absorb RF signals at the desired frequencies. For example, some materials may work well for low-frequency signals but fail to block higher frequencies effectively.
- **Gaps and Leaks**: Even small openings or gaps in the shield, such as seams, ports, or improperly shielded connectors, can allow RF signals to pass through. These leaks can undermine the performance of the shield, rendering it ineffective.
- **Electromagnetic Field (EMF) Coupling**: RF signals can couple through unintended pathways such as cables, power supplies, or other conductive elements. These components must be carefully considered when designing a shielding solution.

1.2. Physical and Design Constraints

In many applications, especially in consumer electronics, the need for compact, lightweight, and aesthetically pleasing designs can conflict with the requirements for effective RF shielding. Thin, lightweight materials may not provide the necessary attenuation, and large shields may interfere with the form factor of the device. Design constraints can also arise from:

- **Thermal Management**: Many RF shielding materials also affect the heat dissipation of a device. Overcoming the conflict between effective shielding and thermal management is often a challenge in electronics design.
- **Aesthetic and Consumer Preferences**: The desire for sleek, attractive products in consumer electronics can lead to compromises in shielding effectiveness. Thin, visually appealing enclosures may not always be the best option for RF protection.

1.3. Signal Integrity and Performance Issues

The process of shielding may inadvertently affect signal quality. In systems where signals need to pass through the shield (e.g., for antennas, sensors, or communication devices), achieving the right balance between shielding and maintaining signal integrity can be challenging.

- **Loss of Signal Strength**: Shielding that is too strong can attenuate or block signals that need to pass through. Balancing shielding effectiveness with signal strength is critical for devices like smartphones, laptops, or wireless communication systems.
- **Interference Between Components**: Components within the device, such as high-speed processors or power supplies, can emit unwanted RF signals that interfere with sensitive parts of the circuit. Shielding must be designed to prevent cross-talk and unintended interference between different parts of the system.

2. Troubleshooting RF Shielding Problems

When issues arise, it is essential to take a methodical approach to troubleshooting. Below are several steps and techniques that can be used to identify and resolve RF shielding issues.

2.1. Conducting Thorough EMI Testing

Before troubleshooting, it is important to first conduct comprehensive EMI testing to determine the source and extent of the interference. This can include:

- **Radiated Emissions Testing**: This type of testing measures the RF energy emitted by the device. It is performed in a controlled test environment (often referred to as an anechoic chamber) to quantify how much RF energy is radiating from the device. This helps pinpoint weak spots in the shield.
- **Conducted Emissions Testing**: Conducted emissions testing measures the RF signals that are transmitted through the device's power lines, cables, or other conductive pathways. It is essential to ensure that no unintended RF signals are leaking into or out of the device through these routes.
- **Field Strength Mapping**: RF field strength measurements can be taken to identify areas of the device or system that have insufficient shielding, helping you locate gaps or leaks.

2.2. Identifying and Sealing Shielding Gaps

Gaps and leaks in the shield are one of the most common sources of RF interference. These gaps can occur around connectors, seams, ventilation holes, and other openings in the device. Identifying and sealing these leaks can be done by:

- **Visual Inspection**: Carefully inspect the shield for any visible gaps, cracks, or poorly sealed joints. The human eye may not always detect small leaks, so visual inspection should be followed by other methods.
- **Using Conductive Gaskets or Seals**: Conductive gaskets and seals are often used to close gaps around seams, doors, and connectors. These seals should be made from materials that are both electrically conductive and flexible enough to maintain contact over time.
- **Ferrite Beads and EMI Suppressors**: In cases where signal leakage occurs through power lines or cables, ferrite beads or EMI suppressors can be added to prevent RF energy from coupling through these pathways.

2.3. Evaluating and Replacing Shielding Materials

If inadequate shielding effectiveness is identified, it may be necessary to reevaluate the materials used. A few common steps include:

- **Conductivity Testing**: Ensure that the materials selected have the required electrical conductivity to block or absorb the RF signals effectively. Testing the conductivity and attenuation properties of materials in a controlled environment can help validate their effectiveness for specific frequencies.
- **Material Thickness and Coverage**: Increasing the thickness or coverage of the shielding material may be necessary to improve attenuation. However, this must be balanced with other design constraints, such as size and weight limitations.
- **Multi-layer Shielding**: In some cases, using multi-layer shielding systems (e.g., combinations of metal and conductive foam or metal and conductive plastic) may provide better results than a single layer of material.

2.4. Addressing Interference from Internal Components

Internal components such as power supplies, high-speed processors, and wireless modules may themselves be sources of unwanted RF emissions. These components need to be shielded effectively to prevent them from interfering with each other or leaking RF signals into the external environment.

- **Shielding Individual Components**: High-emission components should be shielded with dedicated enclosures or shields. Metal cans or conductive plastic enclosures can help isolate these components and reduce their RF output.
- **PCB Layout Optimization**: The design of the printed circuit board (PCB) can also play a crucial role in preventing interference. Careful routing of high-speed traces and proper grounding can reduce the likelihood of EMI.
- **Filtering Power Lines**: Power supplies can be a significant source of conducted EMI. Using appropriate RF filters or adding ferrite cores to power cables can help mitigate this issue.

3. Advanced Techniques for Improving Shielding Performance

In some complex applications, particularly those involving high-frequency or high-power RF signals, advanced techniques may be required to ensure effective shielding. These techniques include:

- **Absorptive Materials**: To enhance the attenuation of specific frequencies, absorptive materials like magnetic or dielectric materials can be integrated into the shielding structure. These materials help absorb RF energy rather than just reflecting it, offering additional protection.
- **Dynamic Shielding**: Emerging technologies such as tunable or dynamic shielding, which can adapt to changing environmental conditions or signal strengths, are also being explored to provide better shielding performance in variable conditions.
- **Shielding with Integrated Filters**: In some cases, it may be necessary to integrate filtering solutions directly into the shielding structure. Combining both shielding and filtering can provide more comprehensive protection against a wider range of RF interference.

4. Conclusion

Troubleshooting RF shielding issues requires a systematic approach, encompassing testing, material evaluation, design optimization, and a thorough understanding of RF behavior. By addressing common challenges such as inadequate attenuation, signal integrity issues, and internal component interference, engineers and designers can create more robust and effective RF shielding systems. As RF technology evolves and becomes increasingly complex, staying abreast of the latest techniques and materials will be crucial to mastering the art of RF shielding and ensuring that devices operate smoothly and safely in an increasingly RF-dense environment.

Chapter 16: Integrating Multiple Techniques: Absorption, Anti-RF, Filtering, and White Noise

As the demand for more efficient and robust RF shielding increases, the integration of multiple techniques becomes crucial. RF environments are complex, with signals coming from various sources at different frequencies and power levels. While each of the individual shielding methods—absorption, anti-RF technology, filtering, and white noise—can be effective in certain scenarios, a comprehensive approach that combines these techniques is often the key to optimal performance. This chapter explores the synergistic application of these technologies to achieve superior RF shielding.

1. The Necessity of Integration

RF environments are dynamic, with interference sources ranging from domestic electronics to industrial machinery and military communications. In such an environment, applying a single shielding technique may not be sufficient to ensure comprehensive protection. RF signals can be absorbed, reflected, or transmitted, and each technique plays a specific role in mitigating these effects. Integrating multiple shielding strategies enhances performance, compensating for the limitations of individual methods and creating a more complete barrier against interference.

By combining absorption, anti-RF technology, filtering, and white noise, engineers and designers can address:

- **Different types of interference**: Absorption primarily targets unwanted energy, anti-RF technology focuses on blocking RF signals, filtering eliminates specific frequencies, and white noise introduces a masking effect to obscure other signals.
- **Wide frequency ranges**: RF signals span a wide spectrum, and different methods are better suited to different frequencies. Combining multiple techniques ensures that both low- and high-frequency signals are effectively controlled.
- **Complex environments**: Devices or systems exposed to varying electromagnetic conditions can benefit from the versatility of integrated shielding strategies. This is particularly true in environments where RF interference is both constant and dynamic, such as in telecommunications, aerospace, and defense.

2. Absorption and Anti-RF Shielding: A Dual Defense

Combining **RF absorption** with **anti-RF shielding** creates a dual layer of defense. While absorption materials help reduce the intensity of the RF signals by converting them into heat energy, anti-RF materials block the transmission of RF waves.

- **Absorption** works by reducing the power of the incoming signals, preventing them from interfering with sensitive components or propagating into other parts of the system. High-performance absorptive materials like ferrites and carbon-loaded plastics are ideal for this purpose.
- **Anti-RF shielding**, such as conductive enclosures, metal meshes, or coatings, works by reflecting or blocking the RF signals from penetrating or exiting the system. When used together with absorptive materials, it provides a more effective barrier by both reducing the signal strength and preventing leakage.

For example, in military applications, where both high sensitivity and secrecy are essential, using a combination of absorption materials inside shielding enclosures and anti-RF technology ensures that even low-level signals are absorbed and blocked before they can cause interference or be detected by external sensors.

3. Filtering with Absorption and Anti-RF Shielding

RF filtering is an essential technique when the goal is to eliminate unwanted frequencies without affecting the desired signals. However, filtering alone cannot address all RF issues, especially when the interfering signals are broad-spectrum or dynamic.

- **Filters** can be integrated into shielding enclosures to allow only certain frequencies to pass through, while blocking others. Filters such as low-pass, high-pass, band-pass, or band-stop can be used to selectively block or transmit certain frequencies.
- By combining **absorption materials** with filters, the system benefits from both frequency-selective attenuation (filtering) and energy absorption. For instance, in power supplies and communication systems, filtering can remove unwanted harmonics or noise, while absorptive materials mitigate broad-spectrum interference.
- **Anti-RF materials** can work in conjunction with filters by ensuring that the shielded areas are not compromised by unintended emissions from connectors, cables, or vents. Together, filtering and shielding form a comprehensive solution that targets both radiated and conducted emissions.

In telecommunications, for instance, this integrated approach is critical when designing devices that must operate in highly congested frequency bands. The filtering ensures that only the necessary communication channels pass through, while absorption materials prevent interference from adjacent signals.

4. Leveraging White Noise for Enhanced Security and Interference Management

White noise is an invaluable tool in RF shielding when used in combination with other shielding methods. It has a unique ability to obscure the presence of specific signals, creating an environment where interference is masked, and signals become harder to detect.

White noise is generated across a broad range of frequencies, mimicking the background noise of an RF environment. This makes it especially effective when the goal is to mask the signals of other devices or communications systems.

- **White noise generators** can be integrated into environments requiring covert operations, such as military or government facilities, to mask sensitive communications from detection or jamming. When coupled with anti-RF shielding and absorption materials, white noise can help obscure signal leakage and reduce the risk of detection by adversaries.
- In **consumer electronics**, white noise can be used in conjunction with RF filters to mask any residual interference. By introducing a background noise floor, white noise can help ensure that minor interference does not affect the performance of sensitive devices, such as medical equipment or hearing aids.
- White noise is also useful in environments where signal clarity is not critical, but the protection of sensitive systems is. For example, in the defense sector, white noise can be used in conjunction with traditional anti-RF shielding to confuse and delay enemy communications and radar systems.

5. Practical Applications of Integrated RF Shielding Solutions

5.1. Aerospace and Defense

In aerospace and defense, RF shielding is critical for protecting communications systems and electronic equipment from external interference or enemy detection. Here, the integration of **absorption materials, anti-RF shielding, filtering, and white noise** ensures a multi-layered defense. Advanced aircraft, for example, employ this integrated approach to protect radar systems, communication equipment, and even onboard weapons from electromagnetic attacks.

5.2. Telecommunications

In the telecommunications industry, devices and infrastructure like base stations, routers, and cell towers are exposed to high levels of RF interference from a range of sources. **RF filtering**, **anti-RF shielding**, and **white noise** are integrated into these systems to ensure signal integrity, protect against interference, and maintain secure communications. The inclusion of absorptive materials helps reduce unwanted signal reflections and electromagnetic radiation, contributing to both system performance and regulatory compliance.

5.3. Consumer Electronics

In consumer electronics, such as smartphones, laptops, and smart home devices, RF interference can degrade user experience and device performance. Manufacturers increasingly use an integrated approach involving **absorption, anti-RF shielding, filtering, and white noise** to improve device immunity to interference and optimize connectivity performance. By combining these techniques, manufacturers ensure that their devices work smoothly in crowded RF environments, like urban centers, where signal congestion is a concern.

5.4. Medical Devices

For medical devices, maintaining precise signal integrity is vital for ensuring proper functioning and patient safety. Systems like MRI machines, pacemakers, and diagnostic equipment rely on the integration of multiple RF shielding techniques. **RF filters** remove unwanted frequencies that could distort sensitive data, while **anti-RF shielding** prevents external interference. **Absorptive materials** reduce the impact of electromagnetic waves, and **white noise** can mask minor interference that may disrupt system performance.

6. Conclusion

The integration of multiple RF shielding techniques—absorption, anti-RF technology, filtering, and white noise—is crucial for tackling the complexities of modern RF environments. Each technique has its unique strengths, and when combined, they provide a robust solution that addresses a wide range of RF interference issues. By leveraging these methods synergistically, engineers and designers can create more resilient and efficient systems that meet the demanding requirements of industries ranging from aerospace to consumer electronics.

As RF technology continues to evolve, the integration of these shielding techniques will become even more essential, allowing for enhanced performance, greater security, and more reliable communication in an increasingly interconnected and RF-dense world.

Chapter 17: Conclusion: Mastering RF Technology for the Future

As we've explored throughout this book, the world of RF shielding is vast, complex, and ever-evolving. The interplay of absorption, anti-RF technology, filtering, and white noise forms the cornerstone of effective RF management. Understanding these techniques and how to integrate them into a cohesive strategy is essential for solving the increasingly complicated challenges presented by electromagnetic interference (EMI) in today's connected world.

In this final chapter, we will summarize the key insights from this book and look ahead at the future of RF technology. We will explore how the concepts of RF shielding are set to evolve, the impact of new technologies on the field, and what this means for industries and practitioners engaged in the design, protection, and enhancement of electronic systems.

1. The Evolving Landscape of RF Shielding

The fundamental principles of RF shielding—absorption, anti-RF blocking, filtering, and white noise—have not changed, but the technologies, materials, and applications have evolved significantly over the years. As RF frequencies continue to expand, particularly with the advent of 5G networks, the demand for more sophisticated and dynamic shielding solutions has grown.

- **Higher Frequency Bands**: With the proliferation of 5G networks and the potential future deployment of 6G technology, new frequency bands are being used for communication. This increases the complexity of shielding systems, as higher-frequency signals tend to be more difficult to block effectively. Advanced absorptive materials and innovative shielding designs will be essential in mitigating the challenges posed by these new RF environments.
- **Miniaturization and Integration**: As electronics become smaller, more powerful, and more integrated, the challenge of shielding devices in compact form factors will intensify. This is especially true for consumer electronics, wearables, and medical devices, where there is a strong drive to maintain performance without compromising size, weight, or battery life.
- **Emerging Threats**: As RF technologies advance, so too does the sophistication of threats to security and privacy. Advances in jamming, spoofing, and RF-based attacks will require the continued development of robust, adaptable shielding solutions that can handle new and evolving types of interference.

2. Innovations Driving RF Shielding Solutions

The future of RF shielding will be shaped by several key innovations, including new materials, adaptive systems, and more efficient design processes.

2.1. Advanced Materials

- **Metamaterials**: Metamaterials, engineered structures designed to manipulate electromagnetic waves in novel ways, have shown great promise in RF shielding applications. By manipulating how light or electromagnetic waves interact with the material, these structures can provide high-performance shielding in smaller, more lightweight formats. Metamaterials could be particularly useful for future 5G and 6G systems, where managing high-frequency signals is crucial.

- **Nanomaterials and Conductive Polymers**: Nanotechnology and conductive polymers are opening up new possibilities for creating flexible, high-performance materials that can provide effective RF shielding without adding significant weight. These materials could be used in applications ranging from wearable electronics to flexible display screens.

2.2. Adaptive Shielding Systems

- **Dynamic Shielding**: The idea of dynamic, tunable shielding that adjusts to changing RF environments is gaining traction. These systems can actively adapt to varying interference levels, adjusting the shielding properties in real-time to optimize performance. Such technology could be employed in applications like defense communications or in environments where interference levels fluctuate rapidly.
- **Active RF Cancellation**: Active RF cancellation systems, which use the principle of destructive interference to counteract unwanted signals, are being developed for specific high-end applications. These systems could significantly improve RF performance in environments with high interference or where traditional shielding methods fall short.

2.3. Integration with IoT and Smart Systems

The integration of RF shielding technology with the Internet of Things (IoT) is expected to be a key development. As smart cities, connected devices, and autonomous systems proliferate, maintaining interference-free operation will become critical. RF shielding solutions will need to become more intelligent, self-monitoring, and adaptive to ensure the smooth operation of IoT networks.

3. The Role of RF Shielding in Critical Sectors

As technology becomes more ubiquitous, the importance of RF shielding across critical sectors continues to grow.

3.1. Military and Security Applications

In the military, RF shielding has always been a cornerstone of operations, protecting sensitive communications and systems from electronic warfare. The increasing sophistication of RF-based attacks—such as jamming and spoofing—requires advanced shielding solutions that can handle more complex and evolving threats.

- **Covert Operations**: The military's need for covert communications systems has made the integration of white noise and anti-RF shielding a priority. As surveillance and counter-surveillance technologies advance, white noise generators will play a significant role in obscuring sensitive signals.
- **RF Protection for Autonomous Systems**: With the rise of unmanned aerial vehicles (UAVs) and autonomous vehicles, RF shielding will be needed to ensure that communication between autonomous systems remains secure and uninterrupted, particularly in contested environments.

3.2. Healthcare and Medical Devices

Medical devices, particularly those used in remote monitoring or life-critical systems (e.g., pacemakers, MRI machines, defibrillators), are sensitive to electromagnetic interference. RF shielding plays an important role in ensuring the safety and functionality of these devices in a world filled with competing RF signals.

Wireless Medical Devices

3.3. Consumer Electronics and 5G Networks

In consumer electronics, ensuring a seamless user experience requires careful management of RF interference. Whether it's a smartphone, laptop, or wearable, users demand uninterrupted wireless performance—especially as 5G networks and Wi-Fi 6 become mainstream.

- **5G and Beyond**: As 5G networks roll out globally, ensuring RF shielding for devices like smartphones, IoT sensors, and even smart cars will become critical to avoid interference and maintain signal quality. RF absorption and filtering technologies will need to evolve to meet the unique challenges posed by 5G frequencies.
- **User Privacy**: With the growing concern about privacy, RF shielding will play an important role in securing devices against unauthorized access and data breaches through RF-based attacks. Shielding solutions will need to adapt to protect devices in an increasingly connected world.

4. Legal and Ethical Considerations

As RF technology advances, the legal and ethical aspects of RF shielding become increasingly relevant. The manipulation of RF signals—whether to block interference, mask signals, or jamming—raises important legal questions.

- **Regulatory Compliance**: Governments and regulatory bodies continue to refine policies regarding RF spectrum management, safety standards, and the permissible use of shielding technologies. Professionals in the RF field must stay abreast of these regulations to ensure compliance and avoid unintended consequences.
- **Ethical Issues in RF Manipulation**: The use of RF shielding technologies in ways that compromise privacy or violate the principles of free communication (e.g., government surveillance, unauthorized jamming) presents significant ethical concerns. The development of transparent and ethically responsible RF technologies will be essential to safeguard privacy and prevent misuse.

5. Conclusion: Navigating the Future of RF Technology

As we move further into the digital age, mastering RF shielding and understanding its applications will be more important than ever. Whether it's designing more efficient consumer electronics, protecting critical communications in defense, or ensuring the reliability of medical devices, RF shielding remains a fundamental component of modern technology. The integration of advanced materials, adaptive systems, and cutting-edge techniques like active cancellation and white noise will pave the way for more efficient, secure, and robust RF environments.

Ultimately, the future of RF technology hinges on our ability to harness and integrate these shielding strategies effectively. By doing so, we can ensure that electronic systems remain functional, secure, and protected from the increasing demands of the modern RF spectrum.

With new innovations on the horizon, mastering the complexities of RF shielding will continue to be a key challenge—and opportunity—for engineers, researchers, and industries worldwide.

Chapter 18: Integrating Multiple Techniques: Absorption, Anti-RF, Filtering, and White Noise

One of the key challenges in RF shielding is not just choosing the right technique, but effectively integrating multiple techniques to create a comprehensive and robust system. In this chapter, we will explore how the combination of RF absorption, anti-RF technology, filtering, and white noise can work together to address complex interference problems. By understanding how to integrate these methods, engineers and practitioners can develop highly effective RF shielding solutions that are more adaptive, resilient, and efficient.

1. The Importance of Integration

In the world of RF shielding, a "one-size-fits-all" approach rarely works. Each technique —whether absorption, anti-RF, filtering, or white noise—has its strengths and weaknesses. Therefore, the most effective RF shielding systems often require a combination of these techniques. Integration allows each technique to complement the others, mitigating the shortcomings of individual methods and ensuring a more robust, flexible, and scalable solution.

For example, RF absorption materials may be effective in reducing reflected signals, but they may not provide full protection against high-power, high-frequency signals. Anti-RF devices, on the other hand, can block specific frequencies, but may not be as effective in environments where interference is pervasive across multiple bands. By combining absorption, anti-RF shielding, and filtering, one can create a multi-layered defense system.

Key Benefits of Integration:

- **Broader Frequency Coverage**: Different techniques excel at blocking or absorbing specific frequency ranges. By combining methods, you can protect against a wider spectrum of RF interference.
- **Improved System Performance**: The combination of multiple shielding techniques allows you to optimize the performance of the system, ensuring that signals remain strong and clear while minimizing noise.
- **Adaptability**: By integrating various techniques, systems can be more flexible and responsive to changing RF environments. This adaptability is particularly useful in environments with variable or unknown interference patterns.
- **Enhanced Security**: In sensitive applications, such as military and communications, integrating multiple RF techniques enhances the ability to block hostile interference, preventing jamming or data interception.

2. Designing Integrated RF Shielding Solutions

To integrate these shielding techniques effectively, it is essential to first understand the specific RF problem being solved. The goal is to create a system that addresses all the sources of interference without introducing unnecessary complexity or cost. Below are key steps in the process of designing integrated RF shielding systems:

2.1. Identify the Sources and Types of RF Interference

The first step in designing an integrated RF shielding solution is identifying the sources of interference. Are you dealing with continuous, broad-spectrum noise or narrowband interference? Is the interference caused by internal sources (like motors, circuitry, or antennas) or external sources (like nearby radio towers or jammers)?

Once the interference sources are identified, you can determine which shielding techniques will be most effective for each problem. For example:

- **Absorption** can be used to reduce reflections and standing waves from internal interference.
- **Anti-RF devices** may be needed to block external high-power signals from entering the protected area.
- **Filtering** can be used to remove unwanted frequencies from incoming signals.
- **White noise** could be deployed to obscure communication signals in high-security environments.

2.2. Layering Techniques for Comprehensive Protection

In integrated systems, each shielding technique works together to address different aspects of the RF environment. Layering these techniques is key to achieving comprehensive protection:

- **Absorption and Filtering**: Absorption materials can be used in combination with filters to target unwanted frequencies while reducing reflections. For example, in a device or room that requires shielding from a wide range of frequencies, absorption materials might be placed on surfaces to reduce reflected signals, while RF filters can selectively target specific frequency bands.
- **Anti-RF Blocking and White Noise**: In high-security environments, anti-RF shielding can prevent external signals from entering, while white noise can be used internally to disrupt any incoming signals that might attempt to pass through. White noise, acting as a form of RF interference, can obscure communications and prevent eavesdropping.

2.3. Material Selection and Placement

Selecting the right materials for each shielding technique is vital to achieving an optimal integrated system. For example:

- **RF Absorptive Materials**: Soft magnetic materials, conductive foams, and ferrites can be placed around sources of internal interference or on walls to prevent signal reflections.
- **Anti-RF Devices**: Metal-based meshes, conductive films, and specialized anti-jamming materials can be applied to external surfaces or integrated into specific components to block unwanted RF signals.
- **Filters**: Both passive and active filters should be used at points of entry for signals, such as antennas, cables, and connectors. These filters should be designed to pass the necessary frequencies while blocking others.
- **White Noise Generators**: These can be placed strategically within a system or environment to mask any sensitive communication or RF signal.

2.4. Testing and Optimization

Once the system is designed, it must undergo rigorous testing to ensure that all shielding techniques are functioning as intended. This involves measuring the effectiveness of each method in blocking, absorbing, or filtering RF interference. Optimizing the placement and balance of each technique will also be necessary to ensure the system is not overly complicated or inefficient.

3. Case Study: Integrated RF Shielding in a Military Communication System

A practical example of integrating these shielding techniques can be found in military communication systems. In these systems, both security and reliability are paramount, and RF interference can have disastrous consequences.

Scenario: A military base is setting up secure communication systems to ensure uninterrupted command and control. The system must be shielded from external jamming signals while also protecting sensitive internal communication.

- **Absorption**: The base's control room uses absorptive materials, such as ferrite panels, to prevent internal signal reflections and reduce noise.
- **Anti-RF Devices**: The building is equipped with external anti-RF shielding materials, including conductive metal meshes and Faraday cages around key infrastructure, to block incoming jamming signals.
- **Filtering**: High-performance filters are installed on communication cables and antennas to remove unwanted frequencies, ensuring that only authorized signals can pass through.
- **White Noise**: Inside the control room, white noise generators are deployed to obscure any intercepted signals and prevent eavesdropping on critical communications.

The integration of these techniques ensures the security of the communication system while maintaining operational efficiency. By combining RF absorption, anti-RF blocking, filtering, and white noise, the military achieves a multi-layered defense against RF threats.

4. Conclusion: The Future of Integrated RF Shielding

As RF environments continue to grow more complex, the need for integrated shielding systems will become even more critical. Engineers and researchers will need to continue refining these techniques, finding innovative ways to combine them into adaptive, scalable solutions that address new RF challenges.

Whether in the defense sector, consumer electronics, or telecommunications, the ability to integrate multiple RF shielding techniques will ensure that systems remain secure, efficient, and reliable in an increasingly connected world. By continuing to push the boundaries of what is possible with RF shielding technology, we can ensure a future where interference is minimized, and electronic systems continue to operate without disruption.

This integrated approach to RF shielding is not just about blocking interference—it's about creating intelligent, adaptive systems that can withstand the evolving challenges of the modern RF spectrum. As technology continues to advance, mastering the art of integration will be key to ensuring the continued success and security of tomorrow's technologies.

Chapter 19: Conclusion: Mastering RF Technology for the Future

As we near the conclusion of this journey into mastering RF shielding, we take a step back to reflect on the intricate technologies, techniques, and strategies that have been explored. From the fundamentals of radio frequencies and their impact, to the various methods of mitigating RF interference—such as absorption, anti-RF technology, filtering, and white noise—this book has delved into the essential aspects of RF shielding. But beyond these techniques, we have also examined the broader implications of RF technology and the direction it is likely to take in the future.

RF technology is not static; it evolves in tandem with advancements in communications, electronics, and security. In this final chapter, we'll summarize the key insights from the previous chapters and discuss the future trends that will shape the RF landscape. The mastery of RF shielding will not only be critical for contemporary applications but will continue to serve as the foundation for addressing tomorrow's technological challenges.

1. The Power of RF Shielding

Radio frequencies are everywhere in the modern world. They are the invisible forces that power communication systems, enable wireless technologies, and affect the functioning of countless devices. However, with this ubiquity comes the challenge of managing RF interference. Whether it's minimizing disruption in military communications, preventing eavesdropping in secure environments, or ensuring seamless connectivity in consumer electronics, RF shielding plays a pivotal role in the effectiveness of RF-based systems.

In this book, we have focused on several core techniques that allow engineers to create reliable, secure, and interference-free systems. RF absorption materials, anti-RF devices, filters, and white noise generators each offer their distinct advantages. However, the real art of RF shielding lies in their integration. By combining these techniques in innovative ways, it is possible to create multi-layered systems that can withstand a wide range of RF challenges—making them adaptable, flexible, and efficient in an ever-evolving landscape.

2. RF Shielding and Its Applications Across Industries

As we've seen throughout the chapters, the importance of RF shielding spans diverse industries, including military, telecommunications, consumer electronics, and healthcare. These sectors not only rely on shielding to mitigate interference, but also to meet stringent performance, security, and reliability standards.

- **Military and Security**: In high-stakes environments, RF shielding serves as a defensive measure against signal jamming and eavesdropping. Techniques like anti-RF technology, integrated with white noise and absorption, are crucial in ensuring the confidentiality and integrity of sensitive communications. The increasing sophistication of cyber warfare and electronic countermeasures makes it clear that RF shielding will continue to play a pivotal role in national security.
- **Telecommunications and 5G Networks**: With the rollout of 5G networks and the increased use of wireless communication systems, the need for advanced RF shielding solutions is growing. The challenge lies in managing interference from the dense array of connected devices, the variety of frequency bands in use, and the high-speed nature of these networks. Advanced RF filters, absorptive materials, and anti-RF technologies will become even more critical in ensuring the smooth operation of these networks.
- **Consumer Electronics**: In the world of smartphones, IoT devices, and wearables, RF interference can significantly degrade performance. Whether it's protecting a smartphone's communication systems or ensuring that a smart home hub works seamlessly without interference, RF shielding is crucial in delivering consumer electronics that function as expected.

- **Healthcare and Medical Devices**: In medical environments, especially those involving life-saving devices such as pacemakers, MRI machines, and other diagnostic tools, RF interference can have serious consequences. Shielding solutions that prevent electromagnetic interference are vital for patient safety and for the proper functioning of sensitive equipment.

3. Legal and Ethical Considerations in RF Shielding

As RF technology evolves, so too must the regulations that govern its use. Legal and ethical considerations in RF shielding are paramount, especially in the context of public safety and privacy. RF interference is not only a technical problem but also a legal one. Governments around the world regulate the use of the RF spectrum to prevent harmful interference and to ensure that signals from different sources do not disrupt essential services.

For instance:

- **Spectrum Allocation**: Governments regulate the RF spectrum to prevent signal overlap and interference. Effective RF shielding solutions must comply with these regulatory frameworks, ensuring that communication networks operate within defined frequency ranges.
- **Privacy Concerns**: As RF-based surveillance technologies become more advanced, there are growing concerns about privacy. RF shielding methods may be employed not only to protect devices from external interference but also to prevent the unauthorized interception of signals.

4. Innovations and Trends in RF Technology

The future of RF technology is poised for transformative changes. With the increasing demand for faster, more efficient, and secure communication networks, RF shielding technologies will need to evolve to meet new challenges. Several trends are likely to shape the future of RF shielding:

- **5G and Beyond**: As we enter the era of 5G and look toward 6G, the complexity and density of RF environments will increase exponentially. New materials and more sophisticated shielding techniques will be required to manage the ultra-high frequencies and the vast number of connected devices.
- **Quantum Communications**: Quantum technologies promise secure, unbreakable communication systems. As these technologies develop, they will likely drive innovations in RF shielding, particularly in terms of protecting quantum communication systems from potential RF-based threats.
- **Miniaturization of Devices**: As devices become smaller and more integrated, the need for compact and efficient RF shielding solutions will grow. This could lead to new materials and designs that offer high shielding performance in miniaturized forms.
- **AI and Machine Learning in RF Shielding**: AI and machine learning are already being integrated into many engineering fields, and RF shielding will not be left behind. AI can be used to predict interference patterns, optimize shielding designs, and even autonomously adjust shielding systems in real-time for maximum performance.

5. Challenges Ahead in RF Shielding

Despite the progress made in RF shielding technologies, challenges remain. These challenges include:

- **Cost and Material Availability**: Advanced shielding materials and technologies often come with a high price tag. Developing affordable, scalable, and efficient shielding materials will be key to widespread adoption.
- **Complexity of Multi-Frequency Environments**: As the number of devices and frequency bands increases, designing systems that can effectively shield against interference across multiple frequencies becomes more difficult. This will require innovative approaches and multi-layered shielding strategies.
- **Evolving Threats**: The threats posed by jamming, hacking, and other forms of RF interference are constantly evolving. Shielding systems must be adaptive and forward-thinking, able to address emerging threats as they appear.

6. Final Thoughts

Mastering RF technology—especially RF shielding—is a critical component of ensuring the reliability, security, and performance of the systems that power our modern world. The ability to effectively mitigate interference and shield against RF threats will continue to be a driving force behind technological advancement across industries. Whether in military applications, telecommunications, or consumer electronics, RF shielding will play an increasingly important role in safeguarding communication systems and data integrity.

By integrating multiple shielding techniques—absorption, anti-RF technology, filtering, and white noise—engineers and practitioners can design systems that are not only effective but adaptive to the ever-changing RF environment. As the field continues to evolve, the mastering of RF shielding will ensure that the technologies of tomorrow are secure, reliable, and capable of meeting the challenges of an interconnected world.

In the future, as RF technology continues to shape our global communication networks, those who master RF shielding will be at the forefront of securing the next generation of technological advancements. The future of RF technology is bright, and mastering its complexities will unlock new opportunities for innovation and progress.

Chapter 20: Closing Remarks and Next Steps in RF Shielding Mastery

As we conclude this comprehensive exploration of RF shielding, it is important to reflect on the key takeaways and provide actionable insights for those who are looking to apply and further develop their understanding of RF technologies. This book has not only covered the technical aspects of RF shielding—such as absorption, anti-RF technology, filtering, and white noise—but has also touched upon the future of RF systems and the evolving role of shielding in an increasingly connected world.

In this final chapter, we will offer guidance on next steps, future learning opportunities, and practical advice for applying the concepts discussed throughout the book. Whether you're an engineer, researcher, or hobbyist, mastering RF shielding requires continuous learning and adaptation to new challenges and innovations.

1. Consolidating Key Concepts: A Review

Before diving into future steps, let's review some of the most important points covered in this book:

- **Understanding RF Technology**: Radio frequencies are the cornerstone of modern communication systems, from mobile phones to satellite communication. RF shielding helps prevent interference, which is essential for the proper functioning of these systems.
- **RF Absorption**: The science behind RF absorption is crucial for reducing unwanted signals. Using appropriate materials for RF absorption can significantly enhance the shielding effectiveness of various devices.
- **Anti-RF Technology**: Anti-RF devices, including jammers and RF barriers, play a critical role in security applications, particularly for military and high-security environments where confidentiality and protection from interference are paramount.
- **RF Filtering**: Filters are the primary tools for controlling the passage of RF signals through systems. Whether it's removing unwanted noise or ensuring specific frequencies are allowed to pass, filters are integral components in RF design.
- **White Noise**: White noise can be used strategically to mask specific signals, making it an effective tool for counter-surveillance and security applications. Its use in interference mitigation offers a unique approach to RF shielding.

2. Looking Forward: Innovations in RF Shielding

The future of RF technology is both exciting and challenging. The rise of new technologies like 5G, IoT, and quantum communications will continue to drive demand for more sophisticated and efficient RF shielding solutions. As new RF frequencies are allocated and new communication protocols emerge, the role of shielding will evolve.

Some future trends to look out for include:

- **Advances in Materials Science**: New materials with improved RF absorption properties will emerge, potentially revolutionizing the design and implementation of shielding materials. For example, nanomaterials and metamaterials may offer enhanced performance over conventional materials.
- **Smarter Shielding Systems**: The integration of AI and machine learning will enable RF shielding systems to automatically adjust to changes in the RF environment. This could lead to systems that dynamically modify their shielding properties based on real-time data.
- **Quantum-Safe RF Shielding**: As quantum computing develops, so too will the need for shielding systems that protect against quantum-based threats. Ensuring secure communication in a quantum world will require entirely new approaches to RF shielding.
- **Sustainability and Eco-Friendly Solutions**: As environmental concerns grow, the focus will shift toward sustainable RF shielding materials. Companies are likely to develop more eco-friendly, cost-effective materials that provide high-performance shielding without harming the planet.

3. Practical Applications and Next Steps

While understanding the theory behind RF shielding is essential, the true mastery of RF technology comes from applying these concepts in real-world situations. Here are some next steps to help you apply what you've learned and continue building your expertise:

- **Hands-On Experience**: If you haven't already, consider building a simple RF shielding setup. Experimenting with materials, filters, and shielding designs will give you practical experience and deepen your understanding of how these techniques work in practice.
- **Advanced Simulation Tools**: Invest time in learning how to use simulation software for RF modeling. Programs like CST Studio, ANSYS HFSS, or COMSOL can help you visualize how different shielding designs will perform under various conditions.
- **Collaborate with Experts**: RF shielding is a multidisciplinary field that brings together materials science, electronics, and communication technologies. Collaborating with experts in these areas can broaden your understanding and inspire innovative solutions.
- **Stay Updated on Industry Developments**: Follow publications, attend conferences, and participate in workshops related to RF technology. The field is rapidly evolving, and staying informed about the latest trends and breakthroughs is crucial for maintaining your edge.
- **Contribute to Research and Development**: Whether you are part of an academic institution or a private company, contributing to the development of new shielding techniques, materials, or applications will help push the boundaries of what's possible in RF technology.

4. Challenges in Mastering RF Shielding

RF shielding is a complex discipline, and mastering it comes with its challenges. Some of the hurdles you may encounter include:

- **Dealing with Diverse Frequency Bands**: RF systems often operate across a wide range of frequencies, and designing a shielding system that works effectively across all bands can be difficult. A multi-layered approach combining absorption, filtering, and anti-RF technology may be needed.
- **Balancing Performance and Cost**: High-performance shielding materials and systems can be expensive. Finding the right balance between performance and cost is often a critical challenge, especially in industries where budget constraints are significant.
- **Compatibility with Evolving Standards**: As communication standards change (e.g., the transition from 4G to 5G), shielding systems need to adapt to new specifications. Ensuring that your solutions remain compatible with the latest technologies is essential for staying relevant in the field.
- **Environmental Factors**: The performance of RF shielding materials can be affected by temperature, humidity, and other environmental factors. Testing under varied conditions is crucial for ensuring long-term effectiveness.

5. Concluding Thoughts: The Road Ahead

Mastering RF shielding is a rewarding journey that requires dedication, experimentation, and continuous learning. As RF technologies continue to evolve, so too will the methods and materials used to mitigate interference and protect communication systems. Whether you are focusing on RF absorption, filtering, anti-RF technologies, or white noise, each area offers vast potential for innovation.

The techniques and technologies discussed in this book provide a solid foundation for those looking to tackle the RF challenges of today and tomorrow. As the demand for reliable, secure, and interference-free communication systems grows, the importance of mastering RF shielding will only increase.

As you move forward in your RF journey, remember that innovation is key. Stay curious, embrace new challenges, and never stop exploring the exciting world of RF shielding. Whether you are working on cutting-edge military applications, designing consumer electronics, or ensuring the security of critical infrastructure, the ability to master RF technology will place you at the forefront of the next generation of technological advancements.

Ultimately, mastering RF shielding is not just about understanding how to block or manipulate signals—it's about shaping the future of communication itself. The road ahead is filled with endless possibilities, and with the knowledge and skills you've gained, you are well-equipped to navigate this exciting, ever-changing field.

Chapter 21: Conclusion: Mastering RF Technology for the Future

As we conclude this extensive exploration of Radio Frequency (RF) shielding, it is essential to recognize the monumental role that RF technologies and their effective management will play in the future of communication, security, and innovation. Through the course of this book, we have covered a broad spectrum of critical RF concepts—ranging from the foundational principles of RF absorption and filtering to the cutting-edge applications of anti-RF technology and white noise in modern security systems. Now, as we close, it is important to take stock of what has been learned and chart a path forward for continued mastery of these critical technologies.

In this final chapter, we will reflect on key takeaways, the broader implications of RF shielding, and the steps you can take to continue your growth in this dynamic field.

1. RF Shielding: A Crucial Pillar of Modern Technology

At its core, RF shielding is about controlling and manipulating radio frequencies to protect sensitive systems, enhance communication clarity, and ensure the smooth operation of devices and infrastructure. The importance of RF shielding has grown in tandem with the expansion of wireless technology, from mobile phones to 5G networks, from the IoT revolution to national security systems. As the use of RF technology continues to permeate all aspects of our lives, from consumer electronics to military applications, the demand for effective shielding systems will only increase.

2. A Deep Understanding of RF Shielding Techniques

Through this book, you have gained an in-depth understanding of the various methods used in RF shielding:

- **Absorption**: The process of absorbing and dissipating RF energy to prevent interference.
- **Anti-RF Technology**: Technologies designed to prevent, block, or alter incoming RF signals.
- **Filtering**: The use of filters to selectively allow or block certain frequencies from entering a system.
- **White Noise**: The strategic use of noise to mask RF interference or create additional layers of protection for sensitive systems.

These core techniques—often used in conjunction—form the foundation of any robust RF shielding system. But this is just the beginning.

3. Integrating RF Shielding Techniques for Real-World Applications

As the world continues to advance into higher frequencies and more complex systems, it will be crucial to master the integration of multiple RF shielding techniques into cohesive solutions. Whether in military, medical, commercial, or consumer applications, the synergy between absorption, anti-RF technology, filtering, and white noise can provide comprehensive protection against interference and ensure the integrity of communication systems.

Case in Point: The 5G Revolution

The rollout of 5G technology represents one of the most significant advancements in wireless communication, but it also brings new challenges. Higher frequencies, more complex networks, and increased device connectivity demand a new approach to RF shielding. Understanding the interplay of these techniques, combined with up-to-date knowledge of the evolving technological landscape, will be key to mastering shielding in the context of 5G and beyond.

Security and Military Applications

In highly sensitive environments, such as military installations or critical infrastructure, the use of anti-RF technologies can prevent eavesdropping and interference from enemy signals, ensuring secure communication channels. The combination of RF absorption and anti-RF systems can be fine-tuned for specific needs—whether that's protecting a battlefield communication network or securing sensitive government data.

4. Looking Forward: Innovations in RF Shielding

The journey toward mastering RF shielding doesn't end here. As RF technologies evolve, so too must our shielding solutions. Looking forward, there are several exciting developments on the horizon:

Advancements in Materials Science

As materials science advances, new materials that can absorb or block RF signals more effectively and efficiently will continue to emerge. This includes the development of **metamaterials**, which are engineered to have properties not found in nature, offering unprecedented control over electromagnetic waves.

Adaptive Shielding Systems

One exciting prospect is the emergence of **adaptive RF shielding systems**, which can dynamically adjust based on the environment. Such systems will use machine learning algorithms to monitor signal levels and automatically adjust shielding properties in real time. This could be particularly useful in complex and changing RF environments, such as urban areas or military theaters.

Quantum Communication and Shielding

As quantum computing and quantum communication technologies develop, the need for RF shielding will expand beyond traditional electromagnetic interference. Shielding techniques will need to account for quantum-based threats, and new methods for protecting sensitive quantum communication channels will emerge as part of the next frontier in secure communication.

5. Challenges and Continued Learning

RF shielding is a complex and multifaceted field, and while this book has provided a solid foundation, there will always be new challenges to overcome. Whether you are dealing with increasingly complex network environments, working to ensure compliance with evolving regulations, or trying to develop more cost-effective solutions, RF shielding will always be a dynamic and rapidly changing field.

Key challenges ahead include:

- **Cost Efficiency**: Balancing the performance of shielding systems with their cost will remain a critical consideration, especially for industries that need to deploy shielding at scale.
- **Environmental Factors**: The effectiveness of shielding materials can vary with environmental conditions such as temperature, humidity, and wear over time. As the need for durable and long-lasting solutions increases, so too will the demand for testing and verification methods.
- **Interference in Dense Environments**: As more devices connect to the same wireless networks, managing RF interference in densely populated environments, such as cities and manufacturing plants, will require increasingly sophisticated shielding solutions.

To overcome these challenges, continued research, innovation, and collaboration will be crucial.

6. Next Steps for RF Shielding Mastery

Now that you have explored the core principles, applications, and future trends in RF shielding, the next steps to solidify your expertise and continue growing in the field include:

- **Practical Experience**: Apply the knowledge you've gained by designing and building RF shielding systems. Experiment with different materials and configurations to see firsthand how different techniques interact.
- **Advanced Study**: Stay abreast of cutting-edge research in RF shielding by attending conferences, subscribing to journals, and engaging in forums that discuss the latest innovations.
- **Collaborative Innovation**: Work alongside other experts in materials science, electrical engineering, and quantum physics to push the boundaries of what's possible in RF shielding.
- **Education and Training**: Consider teaching or mentoring others in the field. Sharing your knowledge and experiences will not only help the next generation of engineers and researchers but will also deepen your understanding of the material.

7. Final Thoughts: Shaping the Future of RF Shielding

As this book concludes, it is clear that RF shielding is a critical discipline for safeguarding communication, advancing technology, and protecting security systems in an interconnected world. Whether you're developing new shielding materials, optimizing filtering systems, or implementing anti-RF devices for secure communications, mastering these techniques will allow you to contribute to a world that depends on increasingly sophisticated wireless technologies.

By continually evolving your knowledge, embracing innovation, and applying these concepts to real-world situations, you will be well-equipped to help lead the charge in the ongoing evolution of RF shielding technologies. Whether in military, commercial, industrial, or consumer applications, mastering RF shielding is not just a skill—it's a crucial step toward shaping the future of communications.

The road to mastery is long, but with the insights and expertise gained throughout this book, you are prepared to navigate the complex world of RF shielding and emerge as a leader in the field. The future of RF technology is yours to shape.

Chapter 22: Appendix: Practical Resources for RF Shielding Mastery

As we come to the final chapter of *Mastering RF Shielding*, it's important to equip you with the tools, resources, and knowledge to continue advancing in the field of RF technology. This chapter provides you with a comprehensive set of practical resources, references, and suggestions to further hone your skills and apply your knowledge in real-world settings. Whether you're looking for academic research, industry standards, design tools, or testing equipment, this appendix serves as your guide to navigating the complexities of RF shielding.

1. Recommended Books and Research Papers

To deepen your understanding and stay current with the latest developments in RF shielding and related technologies, consider the following books and research papers:

Books on RF Shielding and Electromagnetic Compatibility (EMC):

- **"Introduction to Electromagnetic Compatibility" by Clayton R. Paul**

  A fundamental resource on EMC principles, this book offers a comprehensive look at the theory and practical aspects of electromagnetic compatibility, which is directly related to RF shielding.

- **"RF and Microwave Engineering: Fundamentals of Wireless Communications" by Frank Gustrau**

  This book covers the basics of RF and microwave engineering, providing a solid foundation in the design and analysis of RF systems, including concepts on RF shielding.

- **"Shielding of Electronics" by Daryl A. Davies**

  A practical guide for engineers and technicians, this book covers materials, design principles, and methods used in RF shielding and electromagnetic interference (EMI) protection.

- **"Microwave and RF Design: A Systems Approach" by Michael Steer**

  For those seeking to design complex RF systems with built-in shielding, this book provides a systems-level approach to RF design, including shielding considerations.

Research Papers and Journals:

- **IEEE Transactions on Electromagnetic Compatibility**

  This journal publishes state-of-the-art research on EMC, RF shielding techniques, and interference mitigation methods. It's essential reading for staying updated on current developments.

- **"Electromagnetic Shielding" by M. K. Ghosh and S. A. K. Ghazi**

  Published in the *IEEE Transactions on Microwave Theory and Techniques*, this paper provides in-depth analysis of different shielding materials and their effectiveness at various RF frequencies.

2. Industry Standards and Regulations

To ensure that your RF shielding designs meet legal and industry standards, familiarize yourself with the following key regulations:

- **IEC 61000-4-3: Electromagnetic Compatibility (EMC)—Testing and Measurement Techniques—Radiated, Radio-Frequency, Electromagnetic Field Immunity Test**

  This standard outlines testing methods for assessing how well devices and systems are shielded from RF interference, providing benchmarks for EMC performance.

- **ANSI/IEEE C63.4: Standard for Methods of Measurement of Radio-Noise Emissions from Low-Voltage Electrical and Electronic Equipment in the Range of 9 kHz to 40 GHz**

  This standard provides guidelines for measuring the RF emissions from electrical and electronic equipment, ensuring compliance with emissions regulations.

- **FCC Part 15**

  This regulation by the Federal Communications Commission (FCC) governs the allowable levels of RF emissions for consumer electronics in the United States, particularly relevant for manufacturers of consumer RF devices and components.

3. Design Tools and Software

RF design tools are essential for simulating and optimizing shielding systems. The following software packages are industry-leading and widely used in RF and EMC design:

- **ANSYS HFSS (High-Frequency Structure Simulator)**

  A powerful 3D electromagnetic simulation software used for designing RF shielding solutions. HFSS is particularly useful for simulating the behavior of complex RF systems and predicting electromagnetic interference (EMI) in various environments.

- **CST Studio Suite**

  CST Studio offers a complete set of tools for designing and simulating electromagnetic systems. It includes modules for both low-frequency and high-frequency simulations, making it ideal for RF shielding design.

- **Keysight ADS (Advanced Design System)**

  A comprehensive RF and microwave design platform that helps engineers design, simulate, and analyze the performance of RF shielding, filters, and other related components.

- **EMPro (Electromagnetic Professional)**

  A software suite used for the design of complex RF and microwave systems, including shielding, waveguides, and antennas. EMPro allows users to simulate real-world electromagnetic environments.

4. RF Shielding Materials

The right material selection is vital for designing effective RF shielding. Below are some of the most commonly used materials, along with suppliers:

Materials:

- **Copper Foil and Mesh**

  Copper is one of the most effective materials for shielding due to its excellent conductivity and ability to reflect RF signals. Copper mesh is often used in large-scale shielding applications.

- **Aluminum Foil and Mesh**

  Aluminum offers a lightweight alternative to copper and is frequently used in both commercial and industrial applications. Aluminum foil is particularly effective in low-frequency ranges.

- **Mu-Metal**

  Known for its high magnetic permeability, Mu-Metal is specifically designed to shield against low-frequency magnetic fields. It is used in sensitive applications where strong magnetic interference is a concern.

- **Carbon-Loaded Polymers**

  Carbon-based materials are increasingly used in RF shielding for lightweight and flexible applications, such as wearables and consumer electronics.

- **Conductive Fabrics**

  Conductive fabrics combine flexibility with shielding capabilities and are commonly used in applications such as RFID blocking and mobile device cases.

Suppliers:

- **Laird Technologies**

    Laird provides a range of EMI shielding materials, from conductive foils to specialized coatings and films.

- **3M**

    Known for producing high-performance shielding tapes, films, and adhesives used in both consumer and industrial RF shielding solutions.

- **Chomerics (a division of Parker Hannifin)**

    Specializes in EMI shielding products, including conductive gaskets, tapes, and fabrics for a variety of industries.

5. Testing and Measurement Equipment

Accurate measurement of RF shielding effectiveness is essential. The following tools are essential for both design validation and ongoing performance monitoring:

- **Spectrum Analyzer**

    A spectrum analyzer is used to measure the intensity of electromagnetic signals across different frequencies. It helps identify RF interference and verify the effectiveness of shielding.

- **Network Analyzer**

    A network analyzer is critical for testing the performance of RF components, such as filters and absorbers, and ensuring that shielding materials provide adequate protection.

- **Anechoic Chambers**

    Anechoic chambers are specialized facilities designed for testing electromagnetic interference and the effectiveness of RF shielding in controlled environments.

- **EMI Receiver**

    EMI receivers are used to measure electromagnetic emissions and assess whether they fall within acceptable limits according to regulatory standards.

6. Online Communities and Forums

Engage with the RF and EMC community to stay up-to-date and exchange ideas with other professionals in the field:

- **IEEE EMC Society**

  The IEEE EMC Society is an excellent resource for networking, research papers, and professional development related to RF shielding and electromagnetic compatibility.

- **RF and Microwave Engineering Forum (Microwaves101)**

  A forum dedicated to RF and microwave engineers, Microwaves101 provides valuable resources, design tips, and discussions on all things RF, including shielding and interference.

- **Stack Exchange (Electronics and Engineering)**

  Stack Exchange is a great platform to ask questions, share knowledge, and explore specific issues related to RF shielding and other engineering topics.

7. Educational Resources and Certifications

To further your expertise in RF shielding, consider formal education and certification programs:

- **Certified EMC Engineer (EMC Certification)**

    Offered by the International Association for Radio, Telecommunications, and Electromagnetic Compatibility (IARTC), this certification will boost your credibility in the field of RF shielding and EMC.

- **CFA Institute's Continuing Education Programs**

    If you are looking to combine RF technology with financial and investment opportunities (e.g., in the telecommunications industry), consider taking courses related to technology management and investment strategies.

- **Coursera and edX Courses**

    Both Coursera and edX offer online courses in RF engineering, electromagnetic theory, and related fields. Institutions such as MIT, Stanford, and Georgia Tech offer courses that may help further your RF shielding expertise.

Final Thoughts

This appendix provides you with the essential resources to continue growing in your journey of mastering RF shielding. Whether you're in the early stages of designing your first RF shield or you're an experienced engineer working on cutting-edge RF systems, these resources will help guide your path forward. Remember, the world of RF technology is rapidly evolving, and continuous learning, experimentation, and adaptation are key to remaining at the forefront of the field.

By leveraging these tools, knowledge, and networks, you are better prepared to make impactful contributions to the development and implementation of RF shielding technologies. The future of RF shielding is bright, and the mastery of these techniques will be essential in shaping that future.

Chapter 23: Conclusion: Mastering RF Technology for the Future

As we conclude *Mastering RF Shielding: Absorption, Anti-RF Technology, Filtering, and White Noise*, it's clear that the landscape of radio frequency (RF) technology and its shielding mechanisms is complex, dynamic, and rapidly evolving. The comprehensive knowledge shared throughout this book—from the basic science behind RF absorption to the cutting-edge applications in 5G and military defense—has equipped you with a solid foundation to engage in the field with confidence. However, mastering RF technology is not a destination but a continuous journey of learning, innovation, and adaptation.

In this final chapter, we'll reflect on the key takeaways, explore emerging trends that will shape the future of RF shielding, and provide a roadmap for how you can continue to grow as an RF technology expert.

1. The Evolving Landscape of RF Technology

The world of RF technology has seen remarkable advancements, and its influence is only expected to grow. As you've learned in this book, RF shielding is essential in protecting sensitive systems from interference and ensuring smooth communication in a range of applications—from consumer electronics to high-stakes military operations. The challenges of today's RF landscape—such as the increasing demand for high-speed, low-latency networks (like 5G and beyond), security concerns, and environmental impact—require a more integrated and holistic approach to RF shielding.

A few key drivers of change in the RF field are:

- **5G Networks and Beyond**: The global rollout of 5G networks is ushering in a new era of ultra-fast, high-capacity communications. This leap forward will introduce new RF interference challenges, particularly in densely populated urban environments and industrial settings. The push for 5G will require innovations in RF absorption, anti-RF technologies, and filtering to mitigate interference while maintaining optimal performance.
- **The Internet of Things (IoT)**: With the IoT expanding rapidly, there is an increasing need for RF shielding in everyday devices. From smart homes to connected vehicles, RF shielding will play a critical role in ensuring device security and preventing electromagnetic interference.
- **Quantum Computing**: Quantum computing is on the horizon and will require entirely new levels of shielding, particularly for managing extremely sensitive qubit states and minimizing environmental noise that could disrupt quantum computations.
- **Electromagnetic Pulse (EMP) Protection**: With growing concerns about cyber warfare, there is an increasing focus on shielding from high-intensity RF threats, such as electromagnetic pulses. Military, government, and infrastructure sectors are increasingly investing in EMP-resistant technologies.

As RF technologies continue to evolve, the role of shielding will become more integral to maintaining system integrity, performance, and security.

2. The Future of RF Shielding: Innovations on the Horizon

The field of RF shielding is experiencing constant innovation as engineers and scientists develop new materials, systems, and techniques to address emerging RF challenges. Some of the most exciting developments include:

Advanced Materials for Shielding

- **Graphene and Carbon Nanotubes**: These materials are poised to revolutionize RF shielding due to their exceptional electrical conductivity, mechanical strength, and flexibility. Graphene-based materials, in particular, offer lightweight, efficient, and versatile solutions for RF absorption and shielding.

- **Metamaterials**: Metamaterials are engineered materials designed to have properties not found in naturally occurring substances. These materials can be tailored to achieve precise control over electromagnetic waves, making them ideal for novel RF shielding applications. Metamaterials may offer the ability to create more effective, thinner, and lighter shielding solutions.

- **Nanostructured Materials**: Nanomaterials have shown great promise in enhancing shielding performance while being cost-effective and lightweight. Their small scale allows them to absorb or reflect RF signals more effectively, especially in applications where size and weight are critical, such as wearable devices and aerospace applications.

Smart Shielding Systems

In the future, shielding systems will likely evolve from passive solutions to dynamic, active systems that can adjust in real-time to changing electromagnetic environments. These smart shielding systems will be able to:

- **Detect and Respond to Interference**: Using sensors and software, smart shielding systems could automatically detect RF interference and adjust their shielding properties to neutralize it, improving system reliability and performance.
- **Adapt to Different Frequencies**: With the proliferation of 5G and IoT, there will be a need for adaptive shielding solutions that can dynamically tune their properties to block or absorb different RF frequencies. This will help address the challenges posed by the increasing frequency range of RF signals.

Miniaturization and Flexible Shielding

As technology continues to shrink, the demand for flexible, thin, and highly effective shielding materials will increase. Flexible shielding materials, such as conductive films, fibers, and fabrics, will become more common, especially in wearables, portable devices, and flexible electronics.

- **Wearable Electronics**: With the rise of smartwatches, fitness trackers, and other wearables, the need for lightweight, flexible RF shielding will grow. Materials that offer protection against interference while remaining unobtrusive are key to the success of this industry.
- **Foldable and Flexible Displays**: The ongoing development of foldable and rollable screens for smartphones and other devices will also require RF shielding materials that can bend without compromising performance.

3. The Importance of Cross-Disciplinary Collaboration

Mastering RF shielding and its applications is not just about technical expertise in electromagnetics; it also requires collaboration across various disciplines. From electrical engineers to materials scientists, from security experts to regulatory bodies, the future of RF shielding depends on an integrated approach.

- **Collaboration with Materials Science**: As new materials emerge, collaboration with materials scientists will be crucial to identifying which materials are best suited for different RF shielding applications.
- **Cybersecurity and RF Shielding**: As more devices become interconnected, the role of RF shielding in securing data communications will increase. This intersection of cybersecurity and RF engineering will require engineers to understand both the technical and security implications of RF shielding technologies.
- **Environmental Sustainability**: The increasing demand for RF shielding materials raises concerns about the environmental impact of their production and disposal. Engineers will need to focus on the development of sustainable materials and the recycling of shielding components to minimize environmental harm.

4. Preparing for the Future of RF Technology

As an engineer, scientist, or technologist working in the RF space, there are several strategies you can employ to stay ahead in the field:

Continual Learning

The RF field is constantly evolving. Stay current with the latest trends by subscribing to relevant journals, attending conferences, and engaging with online communities. Courses on platforms like Coursera, edX, and MIT OpenCourseWare can provide specialized training on emerging topics like quantum computing or advanced RF shielding materials.

Experimentation and Prototyping

Hands-on experience is invaluable in RF technology. Whether you're designing your own RF shielding system or experimenting with new materials, building prototypes and testing them in real-world environments will allow you to better understand how theoretical concepts translate into practical solutions.

Networking and Collaborating

Join industry associations such as the IEEE EMC Society, engage with professionals through LinkedIn, or attend trade shows and conferences. Building a strong professional network will open doors for collaboration, learning, and career advancement.

5. Final Thoughts: Empowering the Future of RF Technology

Mastering RF technology is not just about shielding systems—it's about understanding the intricacies of electromagnetic phenomena and how they impact every aspect of our connected world. The future of RF shielding will be shaped by breakthroughs in materials science, innovative engineering, and multidisciplinary collaboration. As we continue to push the boundaries of communication, computing, and security, RF shielding will remain a critical area of focus.

With the knowledge and skills you've gained throughout this book, you're equipped not only to address the challenges of today's RF environment but also to shape the future of RF technology. The opportunities in this field are vast and exciting, and the path forward is full of potential for those who are prepared to engage with new ideas, embrace emerging technologies, and adapt to an ever-changing landscape.

May your journey into the world of RF shielding be one of continuous discovery, innovation, and impact.

Chapter 24: Postscript: The Ever-Evolving Future of RF Shielding

As we reach the final chapter of *Mastering RF Shielding: Absorption, Anti-RF Technology, Filtering, and White Noise*, it's important to reflect not only on the technical knowledge gained but also on the broader journey ahead. Radio Frequency (RF) shielding is an incredibly dynamic field that is deeply intertwined with technological progress across industries. While this book has provided you with a deep dive into RF shielding, absorption, anti-RF technologies, filtering, and white noise, the journey of mastering RF technology does not end here. In fact, it is only just beginning.

1. The Expanding Reach of RF Technology

RF technology impacts an ever-growing number of sectors, with new applications emerging in ways we couldn't have imagined a decade ago. As we've seen throughout the book, RF shielding is crucial in industries like telecommunications, defense, medical technology, and consumer electronics, but its potential extends much further. New fields such as quantum computing, space exploration, and autonomous systems are pushing the boundaries of RF technology in novel ways.

- **Quantum Computing**: RF interference and shielding will be critical in the world of quantum computing. The extremely delicate qubits that form the foundation of quantum systems are highly susceptible to electromagnetic interference, meaning RF shielding will be integral to building stable, scalable quantum computers.
- **Space Exploration**: As humanity embarks on deeper space exploration, RF shielding will be needed not only to protect sensitive equipment from space weather (such as solar radiation and cosmic rays) but also to ensure communication systems remain stable over vast distances.
- **Autonomous Vehicles**: Self-driving cars depend heavily on communication systems—such as radar, LIDAR, and V2X (vehicle-to-everything) communications—which will require advanced RF shielding techniques to minimize interference and ensure their safe, reliable operation.

The future of RF shielding, then, will increasingly focus on not just protecting systems from interference but ensuring that systems operate in environments where interference is not just a risk but a fundamental challenge.

2. The Integration of RF Shielding into Broader Systems

While RF shielding has traditionally been seen as a stand-alone aspect of system design, the future will demand more integrated solutions. As systems become more complex, with devices constantly interconnected and communication across vast networks, RF shielding cannot remain isolated. It must work seamlessly with other components like cybersecurity protocols, power management systems, and software applications.

- **Cyber-Physical Systems (CPS)**: In CPS, where the physical and cyber components of a system interact, shielding will need to be integrated within a broader security framework. This will be especially important in critical infrastructure systems such as power grids, transportation systems, and healthcare networks.
- **Smart Cities**: The development of smart cities, which rely on vast networks of interconnected devices, sensors, and communication systems, will require sophisticated RF shielding that can ensure secure, reliable communication while protecting against interference and external threats.
- **Wearable Technology and IoT**: With the growing prevalence of wearable devices and the Internet of Things (IoT), RF shielding will need to address challenges related to miniaturization, mobility, and flexible materials. It will also need to balance performance with user comfort and the aesthetics of consumer products.

RF shielding will no longer just be an isolated component but part of an ecosystem that ensures the functionality, security, and resilience of a system in an increasingly connected world.

3. The Need for Cross-Disciplinary Collaboration

As RF shielding continues to evolve, it will be essential for professionals in the RF space to work closely with experts from other fields. Cross-disciplinary collaboration will be crucial to solving complex challenges and unlocking new opportunities in the RF world.

- **Collaboration with Material Scientists**: New materials, such as metamaterials, graphene, and carbon nanotubes, will be central to the future of RF shielding. Collaboration with material scientists will enable the development of innovative solutions that can provide better shielding while being more cost-effective, lighter, and more durable.
- **Cybersecurity Experts**: With the increasing convergence of RF technologies with digital communications, cybersecurity professionals will play an integral role in the development of systems that protect sensitive data from both physical and cyber threats. Understanding both RF principles and cybersecurity concepts will be critical in designing secure RF systems.
- **Ethicists and Regulatory Experts**: As we continue to see the widespread deployment of RF technologies—especially in sensitive areas such as healthcare and military applications—it is vital that engineers and developers work with ethicists and regulatory bodies. This ensures that RF technologies are used responsibly, with considerations for privacy, data protection, and societal impact.

4. The Growing Role of Artificial Intelligence and Machine Learning

Artificial Intelligence (AI) and Machine Learning (ML) are poised to play a significant role in the future of RF shielding. These technologies will enable smarter, more adaptive shielding systems that can dynamically respond to changing environments.

- **Adaptive Shielding**: AI could be used to develop adaptive shielding systems that learn from environmental data, adjusting their shielding characteristics in real-time to block or filter out interference as it occurs. For instance, AI algorithms could optimize filter parameters, antenna configurations, and even the physical structure of materials to ensure maximum protection against unwanted RF signals.
- **Predictive Maintenance**: AI and ML could be leveraged for predictive maintenance in RF shielding systems. By analyzing data from sensors embedded in shielding systems, AI can predict when a system will need maintenance or when shielding performance might degrade, allowing for more proactive management.
- **Optimization of RF Filters**: AI and ML algorithms can assist in designing more efficient RF filters, allowing for real-time adaptation to signal interference and network congestion. By analyzing large datasets from network traffic, AI could identify patterns and adjust filtering strategies dynamically.

The integration of AI and ML into RF shielding solutions will drive efficiencies, improve system performance, and enable the development of more intelligent and resilient RF environments.

5. Ethical and Regulatory Considerations in RF Shielding

As RF technology becomes more pervasive, it is critical that engineers and developers address the ethical and regulatory issues surrounding RF manipulation. RF technologies have a profound impact on privacy, security, and society as a whole.

- **Privacy**: As more devices become interconnected through IoT networks, the risk of unintended RF exposure and interception of communications increases. Ethical considerations must guide the design of RF systems to ensure that sensitive information is protected and that interference with private communications is minimized.
- **Military and Defense**: The use of RF technologies in military and defense applications raises unique ethical considerations. While RF jamming and anti-RF technologies can be used to secure borders or disable hostile devices, they must be carefully controlled to avoid unintended harm to civilian infrastructure or allies.
- **Environmental Impact**: The growing demand for RF devices will inevitably lead to increased demand for raw materials used in the production of RF shielding materials. Sustainable practices and recycling programs will be crucial to mitigate the environmental footprint of RF technology.

In response to these concerns, regulatory frameworks will need to evolve to ensure the safe, ethical, and sustainable use of RF technologies in the future.

6. Continuing Your Journey in RF Shielding

Mastering RF shielding is a dynamic, ongoing process. As the field continues to evolve, new technologies, techniques, and materials will shape the future. To remain at the forefront, continual learning and experimentation are key.

- **Stay Current**: The RF field is rapidly changing, with new materials, regulations, and technologies emerging regularly. Follow the latest research in RF engineering, attend conferences, and engage with industry experts to stay ahead.
- **Practical Application**: Hands-on experience will be vital in mastering RF shielding. Whether through prototyping or simulations, applying the concepts and techniques discussed in this book will help you refine your skills and adapt to emerging challenges.
- **Collaboration**: The future of RF shielding lies in collaborative efforts across industries and disciplines. By engaging with professionals from diverse fields, you can contribute to innovative solutions and tackle complex challenges.

Final Thoughts

The world of RF shielding is poised for tremendous growth and transformation. With new technologies, materials, and methods, the ability to shield and protect systems from interference has never been more critical. As you continue your journey in RF shielding, remember that the key to success lies not just in mastering existing knowledge but in staying curious, adaptable, and open to new possibilities.

Thank you for embarking on this journey with us. The future of RF shielding is in your hands.

Chapter 25: Appendix: Key Terms, Resources, and Further Reading

As we conclude this comprehensive guide to mastering RF shielding, it's important to provide the tools and resources that will enable you to continue your journey in the field of radio frequency technologies. Whether you're just starting to explore the world of RF shielding or you're a seasoned expert looking to refine your knowledge, this appendix serves as a helpful reference.

Key Terms in RF Shielding and Related Technologies

To ensure a solid understanding of the concepts discussed in this book, it's essential to be familiar with key terms used in the field of RF shielding. Below is a glossary of terms that have been introduced in the chapters:

- **Absorption**: The process by which a material captures and dissipates RF energy, preventing it from reflecting or passing through.
- **Anti-RF Technology**: Devices and materials designed to counteract or block unwanted RF signals. These include jamming, shielding, and filtering technologies.
- **Electromagnetic Interference (EMI)**: Disruption caused by unwanted electromagnetic waves that can interfere with the operation of electronic devices.
- **Metamaterials**: Materials engineered to have properties not found in naturally occurring substances, often used in advanced RF shielding to achieve better performance.
- **White Noise**: A type of random signal that contains all frequencies at equal intensity, often used for RF interference and noise generation.
- **Electromagnetic Compatibility (EMC)**: The ability of electrical equipment to function properly without interfering with other devices or being affected by external sources of interference.
- **RF Filters**: Electronic components used to selectively allow or block specific frequencies of RF signals, either for absorption or transmission.
- **Shielding Effectiveness**: A measure of the performance of a material or device in reducing the amount of electromagnetic radiation that passes through it.
- **Jamming**: The intentional disruption of RF communication by overwhelming the target system with noise or interference.

- **5G Networks**: The next generation of mobile networks, providing faster speeds, more capacity, and lower latency, which brings new challenges and opportunities for RF shielding.
- **EMI Shielding**: Protective barriers or coatings designed to shield sensitive electronic systems from electromagnetic interference.
- **Signal Integrity**: The quality and stability of the signal transmitted through an RF system, which can be compromised by interference, noise, or poor design.

Resources for Further Exploration

While this book has provided a comprehensive overview of RF shielding techniques and their applications, there is always more to learn. Below are resources for further exploration:

Books and Textbooks

"Electromagnetic Compatibility Engineering" by Henry W. Ott

A must-read for anyone interested in understanding electromagnetic compatibility (EMC) and how to design systems that are immune to RF interference.

"Radio Frequency Shielding" by Guy E. Green

This book focuses specifically on the various materials, methods, and design considerations for effective RF shielding, making it a useful reference for engineers.

"Introduction to RF Design" by Les Besser and Rowan Gilmore

A practical guide to understanding RF design principles, this book covers a range of topics, including signal processing, transmission lines, and filters.

"RF and Microwave Engineering: Fundamentals of Wireless Communications" by Frank Olyslager

For those interested in expanding their understanding of RF and microwave engineering, this text offers a solid introduction to wireless communications.

"The Art of Electronics" by Paul Horowitz and Winfield Hill

While not specifically about RF, this classic textbook provides a deep dive into electronic design, with some coverage of RF systems and components.

Journals and Technical Papers

IEEE Transactions on Electromagnetic Compatibility

A leading journal that publishes cutting-edge research on electromagnetic interference (EMI), shielding, and related topics.

Journal of Microwave and Wireless Technologies

Focuses on research in the field of microwave engineering and wireless communications, often featuring papers related to RF shielding and filtering.

Progress in Electromagnetics Research (PIER)

An open-access journal that publishes both theoretical and applied research in the field of electromagnetics, including RF shielding and materials.

IEEE Microwave and Wireless Components Letters

A peer-reviewed journal that covers new advancements in the microwave and RF components, which are directly related to RF shielding technologies.

Websites and Online Resources

IEEE Xplore Digital Library

An invaluable resource for accessing thousands of research papers, conference proceedings, and standards related to RF technologies, including shielding and absorption.

RF Globalnet (

)

A website offering news, articles, white papers, and product reviews on RF and microwave technologies, including shielding materials and systems.

Tech Briefs ( )

This site provides a wealth of articles and case studies on innovative RF technologies, including breakthroughs in RF shielding and absorption.

Signal Integrity Journal ( )

A resource for engineers dealing with signal integrity and interference issues, including RF and EMI considerations.

Online Courses and Certifications

Coursera - "Introduction to RF and Wireless Communications"

An introductory course that covers the fundamentals of RF communications, including the basic principles of RF propagation, filtering, and shielding.

edX - "Electromagnetic Compatibility"

This online course from the University of Colorado Boulder covers the basics of EMC, including methods for shielding and mitigating RF interference in modern systems.

MIT OpenCourseWare - "Fundamentals of RF Engineering"

A free course offering deep insights into RF systems, including coverage of antenna theory, RF filtering, and electromagnetic wave propagation.

CEM Certification from the IEEE EMC Society

For professionals seeking to enhance their qualifications in the field of electromagnetic compatibility (EMC), the IEEE offers a Certified EMC Engineer (CEM) program.

Software Tools for RF Design and Shielding

RF engineers often rely on specialized software tools to design, simulate, and test their systems. Below are some popular tools for RF design and shielding simulations:

- **ANSYS HFSS**: A high-frequency simulation tool used to design and simulate complex RF systems, including antennas, filters, and shielding materials.
- **CST Studio Suite**: A comprehensive simulation software that covers a wide range of RF applications, including electromagnetic field simulation for shielding and absorption.
- **Keysight ADS (Advanced Design System)**: A popular tool for RF and microwave circuit design, including simulations for filters, amplifiers, and RF shielding systems.
- **Comsol Multiphysics**: A simulation software that allows engineers to model the physical phenomena involved in RF shielding, including electromagnetic fields and material interactions.

Industry Standards and Regulatory Guidelines

To ensure that RF shielding technologies are effective and compliant with regulations, engineers must be familiar with industry standards and guidelines. Below are some key standards related to RF shielding:

IEEE Std 299-2006 (IEEE Standard for Measuring the Effectiveness of Electromagnetic Shielding Enclosures)

This standard outlines the methods for measuring the effectiveness of shielding enclosures used to protect sensitive electronics from RF interference.

IEC 61000-4-3 (Electromagnetic Compatibility (EMC) - Part 4-3: Testing and Measurement Techniques - Radiated, Radio-frequency, Electromagnetic Field Immunity Test)

Provides guidelines for testing the immunity of equipment to RF fields and ensuring that devices meet EMC requirements.

FCC Part 15 (Federal Communications Commission - Radio Frequency Devices)

A regulatory framework established by the FCC that governs the permissible levels of RF emissions from consumer electronics and industrial devices.

Conclusion: Your Path Forward

The world of RF shielding, absorption, filtering, and anti-RF technologies is vast and continually evolving. With the resources and key terms outlined in this appendix, you are now equipped to delve deeper into this exciting field. Whether you are seeking to refine your current skills, pursue further education, or apply new technologies, the future of RF shielding is full of potential.

By staying engaged with the latest developments, collaborating with professionals in related fields, and utilizing the resources provided, you will continue to master RF technology and contribute to the creation of more secure, efficient, and reliable systems.

Good luck on your journey in mastering RF shielding!

www.ingramcontent.com/pod-product-compliance
Lightning Source LLC
Chambersburg PA
CBHW082247220526
45469CB00009B/2899